P9-COP-177

WHY WHAT YOU DON'T KNOW ABOUT MEN (AND YOURSELF) MAY BE HURTING YOU:

"All the men I meet are either married, gay, crazy, or just plain boring."

If this sounds familiar, you're probably smart, successful, and still looking for Mr. Right—but in all the wrong places. This soul-searching and provocative book shows you how to confront and change your hidden, love-defeating attitudes and stereotypes. You'll learn the difference between *love* and *longing*. Why it's a good sign when a man stops "courting" you. The best way to get a man to make a commitment. And most important, how to start using your intelligence to create delightful, fulfilling relationships that last as long as *you* want them to.

SMART | FOOLISH
WOMEN | CHOICES

SMART WOMEN FOOLISH CHOICES

Finding the Right Men
Avoiding the Wrong Ones

DR. CONNELL COWAN
DR. MELVYN KINDER

A SIGNET BOOK

SIGNET
Published by the Penguin Group
Penguin Books USA Inc., 375 Hudson Street,
New York, New York 10014, U.S.A.
Penguin Books Ltd, 27 Wrights Lane,
London W8 5TZ, England
Penguin Books Australia Ltd, Ringwood,
Victoria, Australia
Penguin Books Canada Ltd, 2801 John Street,
Markham, Ontario, Canada L3R 1B4
Penguin Books (N.Z.) Ltd, 182-190 Wairau Road,
Auckland 10, New Zealand

Penguin Books Ltd, Registered Offices:
Harmondsworth, Middlesex, England

This is an authorized reprint of a hardcover edition published by Clarkson N. Potter,
Inc., and published simultaneously in Canada by General Publishing Company Limited.

First Signet Printing, March, 1986
23 22 21 20 19 18 17 16 15

 REGISTERED TRADEMARK—MARCA REGISTRADA

Printed in the United States of America

The cases and voices heard throughout this book are real, but names and identities have
been changed for the purpose of confidentiality.

BOOKS ARE AVAILABLE AT QUANTITY DISCOUNTS WHEN USED TO PROMOTE PRODUCTS OR SERVICES.
FOR INFORMATION PLEASE WRITE TO PREMIUM MARKETING DIVISION, PENGUIN BOOKS USA INC., 375
HUDSON STREET, NEW YORK, NEW YORK 10014.

For Casey, Sean, Coby, and Joey
C. C.

For Sara, Eric, and Alexandra
M. K.

Contents

CONTENTS

2 ▪ GETTING SMART

Acknowledgments

We would like to express heartfelt thanks to our literary agent, Joan Stewart, for her abundant encouragement, energy, and infectious enthusiasm for our book. Thanks also to Carol Lacy and Laura Daltry for their sage comments and editorial assistance. And, finally, our gratitude to our editor, Carolyn Hart Gavin, for involving us in spirited and tough-minded dialogues, which ultimately served to make this book as responsive as possible to the needs of our readers.

DR. KINDER: I want to thank my children, Eric and Alexandra, for their curiosity, youthful enthusiasm, and patience while their father worked so many long hours. And to Sara, my wife and best friend, I wish to express my love and gratitude for always being there for me, whether as tough and caring critic or more often as wondrous source of powerful and intuitive glimpses into the mysteries of men and women.

DR. COWAN: To Casey—from whom I learned so much about women, and without whose bordering-on-disgusted, raised-eye-browed, "you really don't get it" looks as a constant barometer I would have wandered more frequently into my male blind spot—my thanks for her support, her outspoken sensitivity to these issues, and her wisdom in leaving me alone to struggle through the writing.

Introduction

Perhaps you are wondering who we are, and why we think we have something to say to smart women about their relationships with men.

We are clinical psychologists who maintain individual practices of psychotherapy in addition to our collaborative work, which began sixteen years ago while we were both completing postdoctoral training at Cedars Sinai Medical Center in Los Angeles. Though trained in traditional psychoanalytic methods and theories, we have also felt a need to develop new ways to both understand and mediate old human dilemmas and "problems in living." It was to realize this goal that we formed a clinic together in Beverly Hills, California, where we dealt with the problems of families in divorce, human sexuality, and male/female relationships.

While this is a first book for us, we have long been interested in the dissemination of psychological information. One of the wonder-

ful, intrinsic rewards of working with someone in individual psychotherapy is the rich
and intense relationship that is established,
but one of the frustrations of individual work
is that in a whole lifetime it is impossible to
touch more than a few people. This book allows us to share with many more people the
struggles and victories of women who have
dealt with difficult relationship issues.

In our individual practices, we have, through
the years, worked with many men and women
who, especially during the 1970s, found their
attitudes and expectations about relationships
dramatically changing, often in ambivalent and
confused directions. We found similar confusions brought to light in our lectures and workshops with men and women. Even though so
much was being written about relationships
and personal development, especially for women,
we kept hearing the same questions cropping
up time and again—questions concerning "love
addictions," the "wrong" men, and the lack of
interest in so-called "nice guys."

In the past ten years most books for women
have been written by women. Yet in our individual work with female patients we discovered that women wanted to hear our notions
and points of view not just because we were
psychologists, but because we were men. These
women wanted to explore their attitudes about

relationships with a man and get feedback from a male perspective.

We write this book not only as psychologists but also as men: sons, husbands, and fathers. This book is written from our point of view: a male point of view. We've tried to be as helpful as possible by making our material as honest as possible. This book deals with issues between men and women—not as they should be, but as they are.

Our book is really all about making relationships between men and women clearer, more realistic, and ultimately happier. We are painfully aware of the tensions between the sexes that have affected us all in recent years, tensions that stem from serious issues and have generated new questions, feelings, and levels of awarenesses. In this transitional era, we all are struggling to discover ways to create and sustain mutually fulfilling love relationships. It is in the spirit of this struggle for mutuality in its most positive form that we write this book.

Who is the "smart woman" to whom we address this book? She is career-oriented and actively involved in her personal development. She strives for a strong identity as a woman and as a person. She has assumed responsibility for the direction of her life. She is confident and values her self-esteem. She is curious about and involved in the changing nature of male/female relationships. Yet she is likely to feel that her love relationships with men are disappointing, frustrating, and very confusing. She senses her choices may be foolish.

We're optimistic, however. We believe there are a lot of good men out there—giving, caring men who deeply want a lasting relationship. As men, we believe we understand how other men think, feel, and react. We're going to tell you about strategies that work with men. We believe that if we can communicate these "insiders' tips" to you, they can help make your relationships less baffling and frustrating, more fulfilling.

Though we initially were cautious about using the term "foolish" in the title of this book, for fear that it might put people off, we knew it fit what our female patients felt and expressed to us with chagrin as well as puzzlement. We believe there is a paradoxical tendency on the part of women today, especially smart ones, to make even greater "errors" with the opposite sex than they might have done in previous years, and there is a very real reason for this. Today, for most women there is a greater gap between unconscious motivations—that is to say, old programming and conditioning—and new conscious aspirations, beliefs, expectations.

There is, in effect, often a clash between the conscious, which has been dramatically influenced by recent social change, and the unconscious, which still may be fueled by those early childhood learnings. It is because of this discrepancy that it is possible for "smart" women to occasionally behave in "foolish" ways.

We further believe that for the mothers of our readers, the central developmental issues were relationship, intimacy, and nurturance. But for those women who matured during the feminist-influenced era, the central issues were personal identity, autonomy, and assertion. Now the issue for most women is the challenging task of reintegrating relationship and intimacy into often very autonomous and career-oriented life-styles.

As psychologists, we believe we can help you to clarify the underlying forces that may be compelling you to make foolish choices. We will try to provide you with a clearer understanding of the ways in which you navigate in and out of relationships.

We're confident that after you read this book, more men, more men who are "right" for you, will look attractive to you. And you'll have new strategies that will work to transform love-defeating patterns into love-sustaining ones.

We ask you in reading this book to be open to the possibility that there are new ways of looking at relationships, and new ways to create and sustain them. There are approaches you can take to create excitement where none seemed possible, and strategies to look beyond male disguises in order to discover the right man for you.

In Part One, "Being Foolish," we will discuss the causes and forces that lead to frustration in romance. In Part Two, "Getting Smart," we will reveal insights and strategies that we hope will convince you that what now may appear to be a stand-off between the sexes can instead be your opportunity to claim delightful, fulfilling experiences with men.

1

BEING
FOOLISH

CHAPTER ONE

Waiting for the Prince

Diane is 28, single, an ambitious and success-ful freelance writer. Most men find her attractive, and she is never without a relation-ship. Yet she always seems to attract men who are independent, self-centered, emotionally closed, and unwilling to make a lasting com-mitment to her.

Diane decided she would like to find a more open, sensitive, and vulnerable man. She thought she had found what she was longing for in Neil. A 30-year-old architect, he was as open and giving as her previous lovers had been aloof and uncommitted. As they grew closer, Neil confided in her about certain career insecurities. He frequently told Diane he cared for her and needed to feel close to her.

Rather than enjoying his openness, Diane found herself pulling away. Justifying her decision, she exclaimed, "I guess I just got bored." Diane is no longer seeing Neil. Sadly, she is once again in a new relationship—this time with a workaholic attorney—that will leave her unfulfilled.

Carla, 42, is a real estate broker who founded a company that now employs thirty people. From the day at age 23 when she experienced the exhilaration of closing her first million-dollar sale, Carla consciously and enthusiastically chose to put her career before a marriage and family. She had been involved with a number of men over the years, but nothing lasting ever developed. Now she finds herself feeling oddly melancholy in her private moments. When she thinks about her past love affairs, she remembers very few joyful moments. She is currently involved with a European film director who she knows is secretly living with another woman.

Samantha, 27, is a junior associate at a law firm. Eric, one of the partners in the firm, was immediately drawn to her intelligence, ambition, and independence. As they dated, however, Samantha went through a metamorphosis Eric found profoundly puzzling: She became increasingly dependent, possessive, and in need of constant reassurance of his love and commitment. Although Samantha's behavior concerned Eric, they continued to see each other regularly, and their relationship grew.

One evening a couple of months later, as they finished a romantic dinner at her apartment for which she had spent hours cooking his very favorite dishes, Samantha told Eric that she wanted to get married, stop working, and have his baby. Shocked by the suddenness of her announcement, Eric began to gradually withdraw from the relationship, leaving Samantha feeling confused and emotionally devastated.

These women are very different from one another. But they share at least one thing in common—they have all made foolish choices in their romantic lives. By choices, we don't mean simply their selection of romantic partners; we also mean how they choose to act with these men.

How many times have you heard these statements, or perhaps even said them yourself at one time or another?

"I always seem to end up with the wrong men."

"If there's one 'rat' in a room full of nice men, I'll find him."

"All the men I meet are either boring or gay. If I'm lucky enough to meet a man who's interesting, warm, and attentive, sure enough, sooner or later, I find out he's married."

"I know it's never going to go anywhere and I know he's never going to leave his wife, but he has this kind of power over me. He walks all over me, and I just let him."

"My relationships always start out great, but something seems to happen that causes the man to drift away."

As psychologists, we hear these remarks every day. In fact, lately it seems there is a rising tide of utter frustration among women concerning men. We became intrigued because we knew these feelings and dilemmas reflect an almost epidemic attitude of disheartening resignation and pessimism.

But women don't simply "end up" with men who are wrong for them. Relationships that have strong initial promise don't sour as a result of inexplicable forces beyond human comprehension or control. Rather, the women who make these complaints have made foolish choices.

We find, so often, that *the more intelligent and sophisticated the woman, the more self-defeating and foolish her choices and her patterns of behavior with romantic partners.* We believe these foolish choices are triggered and perpetuated, in part, by modern, destructively inaccurate myths women believe about men today.

Moreover, women's expectations regarding relationships have been exaggerated by the belief they can "have it all." It is our observation that smart women still look for and hope to find the perfect man—the Prince.

Searching for the Perfect Man

The man I'm looking for? Well, he's got Richard Gere's body, Dustin Hoffman's grin, Lee Iacocca's business savvy, Robert Redford's charm, and Pat Boone's commitment to family. Oh, yes—most important of all, he'll tell me within the first hour that I'm the woman he's been looking for all his life."

Sound extreme? Not to us! We find so many smart women today searching for the perfect man, a sort of Superprince. Of course they know, rationally, that he doesn't exist. Yet often lurking beneath this intellectual understanding is the unspoken but persistent belief that somewhere, somehow, they will find him.

Some women insist that they won't end their quest until they find and capture the heart of this perfect man. But more often, this wish for perfection is hidden behind any one of a number of masks.

Andrea, for example, wears a mask of passivity. At 36, she is still waiting for the "right" man to come along. She can describe him in exquisite detail—his values, his strengths, his gentle, undemanding personality. While Andrea waits, she is "semi-involved" with a married man, one of a long series. She is not in love with him, but the relationship is "convenient." In reality, it keeps her from facing the truth. What she refuses to admit to herself is that even if she actively put herself into situations in which she might meet single, available men, she would be disappointed—her Prince is not made of flesh and blood.

Another way women mask their need for perfection in men is by being overly critical. Elizabeth, who at 28 runs her own graphic design company, considers herself emotionally stronger than and intellectually superior to most men she meets. She always seems to be just ending a relationship, and always for a perfectly logical reason. Each man, no matter how interesting, intelligent, or considerate, is ultimately rejected. Each sooner or later reveals a flaw she seizes upon. Ted, an attorney, was too driven and rigid, consumed by his work. Paul, a newspaper reporter and amateur poet, was "too emotional." At first, Elizabeth was attracted to him for his sensitivity and vulnerability but soon saw him as insecure and weak. Everyone thought Will, a housing developer, would be the one to win her love. She respected him deeply and was strongly attracted to him, and she told her friends, "Will makes me laugh more than any other man I can remember." Yet after a few short months, Elizabeth slowly withdrew from him, complaining he was "not imaginative" in bed.

Although she would never admit it to herself, Elizabeth wants perfection—the flawless man. Elizabeth doesn't perceive herself as overly critical, but simply as a woman who knows what she wants.

While the hypercritical woman is often unaware of how she sabotages promising relationships, the most cleverly disguised searcher for the perfect man is the woman who wears the mask of cynicism. The cynic would object strenuously to being described as someone who's avoiding true commitment until she finds the perfect man. "Men," says the cynic, reciting the story of her latest unhappy affair. "What can you expect?"

Joyce, a 32-year-old nurse, is divorced and has a 5-year-old daughter. During her twenties, she was involved in a marriage that ended in a painful and humiliating way. Her husband had repeated affairs until Joyce's spirit was finally broken and he left her for another woman. As if to try to protect herself now, Joyce looks for the worst in men and unfailingly finds it. Consciously, of course, she vehemently denies that she is looking for anything at all in a man. But behind that denial lies a history of men who never quite measured up. Joyce's search for perfection is so strong, her fear of being disappointed so deep, that she hides her wish for the perfect man inside a shell of cynicism that is all but impenetrable.

Women And Romantic Fantasies

Women tend to romanticize men. From Clark Gable to James Dean, from Frank Sinatra to Elvis Presley, from Tom Selleck to Burt Reynolds, male celebrities have long been the object of female fantasies. Certainly men also fantasize about beautiful or sexy women, but there's a difference. Most men's fantasies are sexual fantasies, and most women's are "relationship" fantasies. Why?

Most adult men today were trained from earliest childhood for a life of action, mastery, and autonomy, whereas women were taught the importance of nurturance and romance. Men tend, as a result, to rehearse and fantasize about what *they will make happen*, while women tend to rehearse and fantasize about things that *will happen to them*. And, most often, these fantasies about the future involve a man, romance, and love.

In workshops with women, we occasionally ask participants to write down their fantasies about men. Invariably, the stories they create include all the standard enticements, situations, and characters familiar to viewers of television dramas or readers of romance novels. There are wonderful chance encounters in foreign settings, elegant restaurants, sun-drenched beaches, and misty morning walks. Then the mysterious stranger is encountered. He is usually unknown, fascinating, magnetic. The woman is swept up in the moment, and the conversation with him is witty, teasing, and seductive. Their eyes lock in visual embraces. Sometimes the woman is the seductress, but usually the man is in masterful control and leads her surely yet gently to the moment of lovemaking. Whether in scented baths or in front of a fire with flames mounting along with their passion, the act of love begins with gentle caresses and ascends to levels of desire and consummation never before experienced.

These fantasies can emerge from the hearts and minds of even the brightest, most sophisticated women. But our point is not that smart women spend their time daydreaming of being swept away by dark and mysterious strangers, or that they have been permanently brainwashed by perfume commercials. Rather, it is that unconscious desires do not necessarily change along with conscious insights and attitudes. And it is the gap between the two that may lead to "foolish" choices.

In many ways, women have been the victims of concerted efforts to shape their beliefs about, and behavior toward, men. Whether the message comes from parents, literature, television, movies, or advertising, the influences are omnipresent. Women have been encouraged to believe that there really is a Prince Charming out there somewhere.

In her landmark book *In a Different Voice*, psychologist Carol Gilligan points out that a woman develops an identity that is a definition of herself, both as a person and more specifically as a woman, while remaining close to her mother. The development of personal identity for a man is quite a different story. A man must separate himself from the mother with whom he has felt so close in order to begin the process of identification with his father. It is for that reason that closeness and relationship are a primary focus for girls during early childhood, while separateness and a push toward autonomy are the normal focus of development for boys.

Thus, Gilligan notes, "Women portray autonomy rather than attachment as the illusory and dangerous quest." In essence, what Gilligan suggests is that most women, despite dramatic contemporary changes in conscious attitudes and behaviors, continue to view independence as uncomfortable and anxiety-producing. It is our belief that the healthy path for women is not to deny this need for attachment but to understand it, put it in its proper perspective, and in so doing, make smart choices in their search for relationships.

Differences in early sex-role conditioning result later on in strikingly different expectations concerning relationships. We all, male and female alike, have a need for novelty and risk-taking. However, while men seem to satisfy this need on the athletic field (or vicariously, watching TV sports) or in the work arena, many women tend to look to relationships for excitement and thrills. This explains, at least in part, why so many women find themselves irresistibly drawn to men who promise a challenge and a sense of intrigue. As psychologists who work with many male clients, we don't find as many men looking for mystery and intrigue in a relationship. And we certainly don't find them looking for danger there; in fact, most men are fundamentally afraid to take risks in the context of a relationship. If anything, men are drawn to women who are nurturing, predictably affectionate, and loyal to them.

Historical Forces Affecting Women

In order to understand some of the forces operating on women today, it's important to review the tremendous changes that have occurred between the sexes in recent years.

The beginning of the 1980s signaled the thaw of the cold war between the sexes, a revival in the perceived value of the importance to the human experience of intimate, committed love. This latest swing of the social pendulum has breathed new life into the importance of relationships and family. Men and women are reconnecting with traditional values and integrating new ones. Here are a few of the comments we have been hearing lately from our women clients and friends.

"I'd like to fall in love, get married, and have babies . . . all those things that sounded so cowardly and provincial a couple of years ago."

"I'm confused. I spent five years getting my master's and I'd like to continue to pursue my career. But I'm 34 now and I realize I haven't had a decent relationship with a man in six years. During that time, my company has moved me to four different cities. It's not that I don't like my work but there has got to be something more."

"I feel as if I'm being torn in different directions. Marriage is very appealing to me, but I'm also aware that there are a lot of obligations that go along with it. There is no question in my mind that I want a baby. I couldn't tell you exactly why; it's just this strong emotional thing that grabs me when I see a mother and a child. I feel I have to have one of my own, but I don't want to become one of those women whose kids are the only highlight of her life. I'm also torn about my job. I enjoy being an attorney, but I know that to do it right takes a huge chunk of time. There just is no way I can do all the things I want to do. Oh, and one more thing. I'm feeling angry that men seem to get to do it all—marriage, family, and career. And the way they do it is by having a wife at home. Maybe that's the answer! Do you know where I can find myself an affectionate, efficient, devoted wife?"

These confusions and strong but divergent forces in women are new. Smart women today want to reembrace many of the truly substantive traditional values without relinquishing the gains of recent years. They are addressing complex questions both within themselves and in their relationships with men. Today they want men in their lives and want to value and feel comfortable with their femininity without compromising equality.

Two decades have passed since the publication of Betty Friedan's *The Feminine Mystique,* which reactivated the long-dormant women's movement in this country. The central thrust of feminism was to free women from the tyranny of sexist education, attitude, and practices. It sought to create meaningful reform not only in the marketplace but also within the context of marriage and family and, perhaps most important, within women themselves.

But, as the movement has continued to evolve, important changes have occurred, most of them involving a reevaluation of the traditional institutions of marriage and family. An unfortunate consequence of feminism was, in our opinion, that it created a myth among women that the apex of self-realization could be achieved only through autonomy, independence, and career. Finding a mate and having a family were secondary goals. In recent years, many women have discovered that, with few exceptions, work is hard, stressful, and not totally fulfilling over the long haul.

Even as we write this book, the wariness women have felt toward men during the last decade continues to diminish. Yet women are still concerned about becoming overly dependent on men or obsessed with them. And, we might add, these are legitimate concerns.

Anna, a 33-year-old public defender who has

never married and whose only live-in relationship, two years long, ended three years ago, says, "I have done all the 'dating' I want. I'm ready to find someone, get married, buy a house, and have a baby—in that order, and with lightning speed. But I've noticed something curious about how I relate to men. I've met some terrific guys, but as much as I've liked them, I'm also aware of waiting for them to screw up in some way. It's as if I don't want them to be all that important in my life."

We believe that a new era is now emerging for both women and men. The prized independence of the autonomous and divorced all too frequently pays off in loneliness, economic woes, and regret. While marriage might carry along with it new forms of obligation, it also promises new forms of freedom and fulfillment. Children can be incredibly taxing and exhausting, but they're magical and rewarding in ways that deepen and complete their parents' lives.

The women's movement gave women a sense of options and a clearer vision of their own worth and potential. It made them aware that their needs were important, that they could and should make important decisions about the quality and structure of their lives. But women today also want to establish love relationships with men. With that in mind, they are abandoning the residues of anger and distrust of men and are establishing relationships on more consciously and more clearly negotiated footings of equality. They are feeling a greater acceptance of their own capacity for love and nurturance, and are experiencing the biological and emotional drive to have children.

More and more, we believe, smart women are discovering that self-fulfillment cannot be realized through career and self-mastery alone. Neither can it be gained through love alone. Self-realization comes from the achievement of both love and mastery.

CHAPTER TWO

Daddy's Little Girl

A woman's wish for the perfect man has its roots in early childhood experiences, particularly the relationship between father and daughter. Fortunately, the women's movement has exposed the subtle yet harmful mechanisms and effects of sexist parenting; nevertheless, most single women between the ages of 25 and 45 were likely reared by parents with traditional attitudes and sex-role biases.

Ordinarily, there exists a natural and healthy affinity between girls and their fathers. But many women had overly solicitous and dependent relationships with their fathers that created an emotional connection with them that is hard to break. They loved their daddies, wanted to please them, and most especially wanted to be loved back. Although their brothers were pressured to become gradually more and more independent, they were not. Their fathers loved the feeling of protectiveness they had for a daughter. They loved helping her and even may have felt rejected and unneeded if she rebuffed an offer of assistance or "rescue." The same men who conscientiously taught their sons how to prevail in difficult situations traditionally cautioned their daughters to avoid such situations. Most often, fathers rewarded a daughter for being sweet, obedient, and passive and a son for being strong, adventurous, and aggressive.

Mothers, for their part, further influenced their daughters' attitudes toward independence through the examples they set and by their interaction with the father. Some women were fortunate to have mothers who communicated a sense of comfort with their own independence and a feeling of confidence and mutuality in dealing with their mates. Other, less fortunate women had maternal role models who communicated feelings of fear and anxiety associated with independence and who had a tendency to be overly deferential to their mates. These mothers found it hard to push their daughters to do the very things they themselves were afraid to try, so the pattern of fear and dependency was perpetuated in another generation. Essentially, dependent mothers unconsciously taught their daughters to look for a man to do the risk-taking and to protect and watch over them.

Paula, a woman in her mid-twenties, relates, "My mother always gave in to my father. He made all the decisions. She had to ask him for money and get permission to buy even little things. My mother looked to my father for everything." Paula became a younger version of her mother and has looked for a man to provide "everything." Had Paula's mother been more self-assured and in possession of a greater sense of entitlement for her own needs and personal rights, she might not have let Paula's father be such a unilaterally controlling force in the family. In turn, Paula would have had a more balanced role model who communicated a sense of confidence and pride in being a woman.

Sydney, a 34-year-old graphics designer, describes her childhood: "I learned to fend for myself early and like it. My mother worked for as long as I could remember, and while neither she nor my dad had a terrific job, they always seemed to enjoy each other and worked as a team. Mom had her own interests and separate activities, and Dad not only respected that but encouraged her—maybe it made him feel more comfortable pursuing the things he enjoyed himself. I never thought of being anything other than independent when I grew up; that was simply the way everyone in our family was, and we all enjoyed it. I can remember as a kid trying to coax my parents to do things for me that were hard. Sometimes if I was really over my head they would step in, but otherwise they pushed me to just struggle through. I hated it at the time, but from this perspective I know it made me a lot stronger, and I like feeling strong." Fortunately, Sydney had the kind of loving and self-contained models at home that help a woman create and feel secure within an autonomous life-style.

Leigh, a 32-year-old architect, was the youngest child in a family that included four older brothers. Hers was a traditional upbringing; she had a working, responsible, and caring father and a mother whose entire identity and range of activities centered upon the needs of her large and active family. The support and love Leigh received from her family helped create the confidence and self-esteem so necessary to meet the challenges she took on and mastered. It wasn't so much that challenge was frightening as it was the fear of dependency and fading personal identity she associated with family and tradition.

As Leigh recalls, "I remember when I was

15 or 16 and Mom was in her early forties, my brothers were all leaving home, working or going to school. I was busy with my own friends, and none of us had time for Mom any longer. I remember her as being very depressed and lonely—she had devoted herself to us totally and when we didn't need her anymore, her whole sense of purpose in life was stripped away. It made me feel terrible, and I made up my mind that I would never let that happen to me."

Leigh graduated from college with honors and went on to study architecture and start her own thriving business. Leigh notes, "I certainly became independent, so much so that I felt I didn't need a man—or I guess marriage, more accurately—for anything, money, security, sex. I really have enjoyed what I've accomplished, but lately I've felt a growing need to settle down. I would like to get married, take some time off from work, and have children. But I'm afraid that if I let myself need somebody or let someone need me I'll lose my ability to be in control and feel self-contained." Leigh's mother wasn't bad or inadequate; she tried to do what she felt was best for her children. The problem is simply that the world has changed, and Leigh's inheritance from her mother has become anachronistic and therefore confusing.

Learning to Be Cute

All children fuss and cry when they are lonely, wet, or hungry. Crying is not a self-conscious response in very early infancy, but children soon learn to use it to consciously manipulate those around them. They learn that if they cry loud enough and long enough, they usually can elicit a reaction from their parents. Crying is a powerful tool, but essentially a negative one—not very enjoyable either for the child or for the child's parents.

Cuteness, on the other hand, is a child's first positive source of power and leverage. Parents love it, and so does the child. Being cute gets children attention and affection. Cute is vulnerability made charming. Cute wins a smile, a quick hug, approval. Cute gets its way. But it is indirect and based upon manipulation of someone else's feelings and actions.

At an early age, cute is captivating in both girls and boys. But when children brought up in traditional, sex-stereotyped households reached the age of four or five, something quite different began happening to boys. Cute behavior began to be subtly, and sometimes not so subtly, discouraged in boys and encouraged in girls. Many fathers in particular openly reveled in the coy and helpless manner that their daughters employed with them. Girls loved being able to make their fathers melt, and they learned to push all the right buttons. They were able to make Dad feel powerful and giving and enhance the feeling of maleness he associated with being a father. As time went on, these girls learned to act this way whenever a man was present, a behavior pattern often unconsciously passed on from mother to daughter. Many women tell us they have noticed in talking to a woman friend that the woman changes when a man comes into the room. It's not solely what is said or not said, but a host of nonverbal behaviors, postures, and styles of communicating. Such behaviors are often sexually seductive—they're a reaction to a male presence and are directed toward gaining attention and approval from the man.

Learning to Be Indirect

Laura, an only child born to a professional couple in their late thirties, learned as a little girl never to be direct with her father. Even though she loved and needed him, she felt a vague but persistent fear whenever she dealt directly with him. Her father was ill-tempered and controlling in his relationships with his wife and daughter. In reality, there was little in his life he could actually control, with the exception of Laura, so he wasn't about to relinquish his short leash on her. In turn, she learned how to humor and manipulate him. She could extract pretty much whatever she wanted from him without ever having to be direct. Over the years, Laura came to dislike and distrust her father as a result of his inability to handle personal communication that was direct and honest.

These feelings and behaviors, unfortunately, have contaminated the intimate relationships she has had as an adult. She finds she is not very trusting of men and tends to be indirect in her own communications. Sadly, Laura isn't unique in her distrust of the safety and effectiveness of being open with men. Many girls learned similar patterns of negotiating their needs—not out of choice or desire but because that was the communication pattern observed between parents or because being indirect was the only successful means of getting what they needed. How do these patterns develop? Some are learned by girls from their mothers.

Sandy describes her mother as "always able to get just what she wanted from Dad." She recalls, "I think she probably could have gotten the same thing just by asking or telling him what she wanted. But she never did. It always seemed like a game to her. I think she really enjoyed getting him to do things without knowing he was being positioned. I ended up thinking he must be pretty dumb not to see what she was doing."

Karen saw her mother as weak around her father. "Mom would put on this helpless front when Dad was around. It was a real routine. She got him to do all the things she didn't want to do herself. She called him 'Daddy,' especially when she was about to do one of her numbers on him. It's kind of funny, but when he wasn't around, she was tough as nails—she could do anything."

Karen says, "I didn't really understand it until I was older, but Mom was very clever when it came to my father. She was either all over him in a fake affectionate way or cold and cutting. She was all promise or threat, depending on what she thought would work best."

Fortunately, many women had mothers who communicated more openly and directly with their mates, providing models of communication that were clear and devoid of the painful and humiliating disguise of indirectness. In turn, such women bring those same patterns of communication into their adult male/female relationships. The mothers of many women, however, believed it necessary to be indirect in the expression of their needs and wishes and inadvertently passed on that lesson to their daughters.

Children have no way of judging whether behaviors are healthy and justified or distorted and inappropriate. They simply observe and learn. Boys learn how to be a man and girls learn how to be a woman from the like-sexed parent. This process, called "identification" or "modeling," is virtually automatic. A young girl doesn't ask herself, "Are there other ways of being a woman than what I see in my mother, or is this how all women get what they want from men?" Later, such questions do emerge, but often after the most fundamental and lasting aspects of the identification process have occurred.

Women blessed with mothers who related to their husbands in clear and direct ways are fortunate:

Carla, a 30-year-old pediatric resident, grew up in a tiny town in Arizona. The oldest of five children, Carla learned responsibility at an early age, for she helped care for the other children. Her father was an immigration officer, and her mother not only ran the household but had a time-consuming bookkeeping job for several local businesses as well. Neither of her parents had much formal education, but learning was a highly valued and emphasized part of the day-to-day life of her family. There was little extra money for luxury items, but, as Carla notes, "My mother was a voracious reader—everything from trashy novels to philosophy. Books were treasures in our house, and I can't ever remember wanting one I didn't get. We used to pass books around from person to person, and even though my dad didn't read all that much himself, he always joined in our lively discussions and always seemed to have a strong opinion. Looking back, Mom was much more literate, much more the intellectual, but she had a respect and affection for my dad that was consistent through the years of my childhood. And he—well, Dad simply adored her. Even though he died when I was 16, I think it was seeing them together that really let me like and trust men. I mean, not only did she love him fiercely, which was very apparent, but she liked him—she thought he was funny; she even enjoyed the kind of tough, macho, volatile parts of him that were such a contrast to her gentleness and consistency. Mom was always straight with Dad— even on touchy subjects or when he didn't really want to hear what she had to say. Sometimes he would react and it could get pretty heated, but I know he respected and appreciated her honesty and liked how spunky she was with him."

Carla, as an adult, genuinely likes men. She

is neither intimidated by them nor hesitant to be assertive when necessary or loving when she feels like it.

It is not just the mother who shapes styles of influencing. Manipulative techniques have also been taught and reinforced by fathers, although rarely intentionally or consciously. Many men tolerated, and some even secretly enjoyed, being manipulated by a daughter. Flattered by her helplessness, they felt protective, strong, and needed, the most powerful emotions in that mysterious link between father and daughter. Many a father found himself doing things for his daughter which, under similar circumstances, he would force a son to do on his own. This model of the ever-handy, always-willing father has conditioned many girls to seek the same traits in their mates.

Lynn grew up in a lower-middle-class family. She was the only girl, the baby of the family, and the darling of her father's eye. Both parents focused their attention and adoration on Lynn, whose accomplishments were to go beyond anything the parents hoped to achieve personally. Her father was particularly doting, giving her the material things he thought befitting his "little princess." Lynn's bedroom was decorated and furnished far beyond the means of the parents and in sharp contrast to the rest of the apartment. Her father saw to it that she bought her clothes at only the finest stores. He even drove her across town each Sunday so she could attend church in a wealthier suburb. The more he gave, the more she wanted and the more she got. It's no wonder that "little Lynnie" grew into a voracious adult.

Initially warm and adoring with men, Lynn quickly became demanding and critical of anything less than the Herculean effort put forth by her father. She was absolutely determined to find a man who would also think, "There's nothing too good for my baby."

Lynn didn't *hope* men would give and do for her, she *expected* them to, without reservation, and without any realistic consideration on her part of the man's individual circumstances.

Finally, when Walt, a kind and very traditional man, proposed to her with proper ceremony and a sizable diamond ring, Lynn gave him a qualified yes. Lynn did get married, but she has never received the fuss and adoration she was led to believe she deserved. Her husband's resentment only increased as her demands mounted. Lynn's unrealistic expectations have led to chronic disappointment for her, and for Walt, a nagging feeling of inadequacy.

Obviously, the healthy, caring father is concerned about his daughter's view of men. He doesn't allow his own needs for control and/or adoration to overly influence his behavior toward his daughter. He wants her to grow up as strong and capable as possible. With growing enlightenment, we're seeing more of these positive father-daughter patterns emerging.

The Powerful Father

Another pattern that results from the powerful connection between girls and their fathers is the problem of overidealization. Sometimes the father truly is a hard act to follow. Alice's father, for example—a handsome, dignified, successful doctor—made for difficult competition. No matter how hard Alice tried not to, she always ended up comparing her boyfriends to her father. Somehow, the boyfriends always came up short. Her father is large enough in real life, but to Alice he is even larger because she views him through the eyes of an adoring daughter.

Sara's mother died soon after Sara was born. Sara was raised by her father, a dynamic, temperamental, and frequently tyrannical movie producer. Sara was in awe of him. As an adult, she has become disdainful of men who don't possess her father's aura and power. This unfortunately narrows tremendously the range of men she sees as potentially suitable for her as mates.

Often it is hard for women to break away from powerful fathers. A woman doesn't free herself from bonds of dependency simply by removing herself from her father's physical presence. Going away to school or getting an apartment or a job does not necessarily change a woman's wish to be taken care of. That need is simply transferred to the "new man" in her life.

Breaking free of that dependent tie requires confronting and overcoming fears of independence, working through the anxiety that inevitably accompanies the process of becoming independent. It also requires a more realistic acceptance of men as they are, not as childhood fantasies would like them to be.

The Missing Father

Women who have had an incomplete relationship with their fathers or no relationship at all have been deprived of normal experiences and expectations. These experiences are necessary to be able to clearly separate reactions toward the father from reactions to men in general. What effect does not having had the experience of a father's love have upon the way these women view men as adults?

The concepts of the father and the mother

are profoundly primitive and powerful. When a girl lacks a father in her life, she creates a fantasy father. The fantasy is constructed from watching TV and movies, reading books, and observing other children's fathers. Bit by bit, a composite father takes form. The image that emerges is composed of the most interesting, comforting, and loving of elements. The fantasized, wished-for father is invariably strong and protective.

Such wishful dreaming is healthy in that the girl is nourished, to some degree, by the vision of what a good father could be. But there are often distortions. Rarely is there any acknowledgment of possible flaws.

The powerful longing for the father and his love often leads a woman to continue the search into adulthood. Anita, who at 34 has sadly not yet been able to sustain a happy, lasting relationship with a man, revealed, "My father died when I was two but I always had an idea of exactly what he was like. I dreamed about him as I got older. He would come in and help me or save me from something bad. I knew that if only he were around, I'd feel safe."

Anita's fantasy about her father has caused real interferences with men. She hasn't yet found anyone with whom she feels "safe," whom she can trust not to abandon her as her father did. In addition, the men she has been with haven't lived up to the image she constructed so long ago of what a man should be.

The Unresponsive Father

Lonnie describes her father as a "blob." "He was there, but we never really talked and he wasn't interested in me or what I was doing. I guess you could say we had a nonrelationship. Nothing really bad happened, but what was bad was just that—nothing at all happened."

The men Lonnie is attracted to are flamboyant, larger than life. She says, "I keep on needing something dramatic, alive, in men. Well, I've had my share of dramatics. These guys are flashy and exciting at first but not much beyond that. I know they aren't what I need, but I keep picking them. I guess I'm just scared of getting stuck with a man like my dad."

Nancy, a 34-year-old legal secretary, loved her father and desperately needed his love in return. He was a preoccupied man—withdrawn and unaffectionate. Nancy recalls trying to hug her father for the last time when she was 11.

"It was his birthday. My mother let me stay up late to wait for him—he was just getting back from some business trip. When he came in the door, I ran to him and hugged him, but he just pushed me away. I guess he was always uncomfortable with affection. When I was older, my mom told me they had a lousy sex life."

As a girl, Nancy could never understand why her love for her father wasn't returned. "I kept wondering what was wrong with me and I kept trying to be a better girl, to win his love." She is still trying to be a "better girl" —wanting now to please the men she goes out with in an attempt to win their love. Unfortunately, her overeagerness to please, her naked hunger for affection, sends men running—and not in her direction.

Linda's father was an alcoholic who neglected not only her but the entire family. "I could never count on him," she says. "He was terrific when he was sober but very mean when he got drunk. I never felt secure even during good periods. He was never really able to take care of us." Now a 39-year-old shop owner, Linda has difficulty trusting men. She sees all men as being as ungiving and unstable as her father was. So desperate is she to feel safe and cared for, and so angry is she about what her childhood lacked, that she pushes men away before they get the opportunity to let her down or disappoint her in any way.

Searching for the father's lost love is a distinctly losing activity. No man, no matter how much he would like to, can make up to a woman what she lacked as a child. That kind of love can only be given to a child by a parent. Longings of this nature are seldom consciously defined. Women who engage in this quest know only that they always end up feeling disappointed by men—but it's not because the men they choose are inadequate. It's because their expectations are distorted.

The Secret Need
to Be Rescued

Many women, no matter how strong or competent, have a secret need to be rescued. Little girls, as we have noted, are not traditionally encouraged to become autonomous. They're taught to get help rather than to help themselves. As Lavonna recalls, "I always counted on guys to help me when things got tough. I never realized how helpless it made me seem and, I guess, be."

Lavonna learned to ignore her own problemsolving skills and instead rely on skillfully maneuvering a man to assist her. While men were learning to directly confront and solve life's challenges, Lavonna was learning how to get men to "rescue" her. The men gained experience with handling problems, while she learned how to "handle" the men.

The overprotective father may think he is merely being a loving father, but he is really teaching his daughter that she needs his protection. As an adult, she is likely to seek out men who provide a similar sense of security and protection.

What is perhaps most dangerous about rescue fantasies is that they usually are not conscious. Women know intellectually that they can't be "rescued" and sheltered from life's risks and insecurities. But this seductive fantasy is nonetheless surprisingly prevalent. And it operates as a kind of radar, homing in on the kind of man this woman picks: "rescuers." So often in the course of psychotherapy we hear even the most accomplished and savvy women express the wish to be taken care of or rescued from their burdens.

Here is the problem: We all want to be taken care of, nurtured, and loved. But we must look to ourselves for some of this nourishment. Unfortunately, all too often, women have been taught to fulfill these needs through mate selection. A mate should be more than a solution to a problem.

Only a clear understanding of early experiences with a father will enable women to free themselves from unconscious expectations that can cause problems in adult relationships with men. Failure to achieve a separation from the father can cause deep conflicts and sabotage even the most promising relationship.

CHAPTER THREE

How Men Respond to Daddy's Little Girl

Men really do prefer women who aren't as strong or intelligent as they are, right? Wrong! But many women believe this common myth. It's almost an article of faith that men will melt under the spell of cute, sweet, adoring, childlike women. In this chapter we'll show you how men respond to these traits in women and what happens to relationships when the woman has not abandoned the role of "Daddy's little girl."

Helplessness

We've already discussed how the unfortunate behavior patterns of helplessness and indirect communication of needs become established in girls and the ways in which those behaviors may be enjoyed and reinforced by fathers. As girls become women, it's only natural that some continue to use these same patterns to get men to respond warmly to them. Initially, men can find helplessness on a woman's part fun, flattering, and attractive. It builds in a comforting pad of safety in the beginning stage of a relationship because it allows the man to feel as if he is in control.

Ben, an architect in his mid-thirties, has been divorced for nearly a year after an eight-year marriage. He describes his feelings about Cindy, a woman he has been dating for two months:

"It was just great when I first met her. Maybe it was the welcome contrast with my ex-wife, but I loved how soft and feminine Cindy was. She made me feel strong and protective, which was great after my wife walked out on me for supposedly being an egocentric, unfeeling bastard.

"But I've got to tell you, it's wearing a bit thin. I know there's more to her, but I just don't know how to find it. Though I really do like a lot of things about her, now when I talk to her on the phone, it's beginning to sound like baby talk."

Cindy cares a great deal for Ben, and, in fact, she is much stronger than she seems. Her father doted on her, especially when Cindy was in apparent need of his strength and protection, and she plays out these early learning patterns unconsciously with the men in her life—selling out her considerable real strength and competence and ultimately driving away the men she wants in the process.

What Ben has found is that he needs someone who is more grown-up and less "helpless." What at first allowed him to feel safe and valued now causes annoyance and resentment.

Men don't resent helplessness in a child or a young daughter; it's appropriate. But men do resent helpless women. First, helplessness creates excessive demands on men, as we'll explain shortly. Second, men may envy women's greater freedom to indulge their helplessness, something which is socially forbidden to men.

Barry, a junior high school science teacher, speaks for many men when he says, "I don't want a woman to pat me on the back and then sit back and expect me to do everything. I need a real partner, not a little girl to take care of. What about me? Who's going to comfort me when I feel hassled?"

Most men are not looking for a surrogate daughter or someone to pump up their egos. Today, more than ever, they are looking for partners. It's important to recognize that men have strong dependency needs of their own.

When a woman appears helpless, the man often views her as someone who may not have the capacity to satisfy his needs for nurturance.

For women who use childlike behavior as a dominant strategy in their relationships with men, their "perfect" man is always some variation of the ever-adoring father. Whether or not the men are in fact fatherly or adoring, these women perceive them as such.

Game-Playing

In Chapter Two, we described the ways in which children learn to get what they need from their parents. However these styles of manipulation are learned—from one's mother or father—they definitely can prove disastrous when expressed in adult man/woman relationships.

When a child grows up feeling that manipulation is necessary for getting what he or she wants, it's very unfortunate, for the adult can become caught in an intricate web of veiled threats and poses of helplessness. What's saddest is that whenever we achieve anything in an indirect way, we feel bad inside—such victories are hollow and don't really enhance our confidence or self-esteem.

Still another legacy of this game-playing for

women is the fear and basic distrust of men it creates. Women cannot be truly comfortable with men if they try to "handle" them in indirect ways, backing into important discussions and not expressing their needs and desires openly and directly.

"I don't think she's ever going to be convinced that I love her," says Lorenzo, 31, an assistant district attorney who has been living with Christina, 27, a court reporter, for the past year. "She's always putting me through these little tests. Like asking me to take off work early to pick up her dog at the vet right as I'm preparing for a major trial. And I find myself having to account for all of my time to her. I know she doesn't really suspect me of anything, it's just her need to keep tabs on me. She is wonderful in so many ways, but her insecurity is beginning to get to me. When she went away for a week to visit her parents, I felt so relaxed. I know she wants to get married, but I can't imagine having to play these endless games and give her proofs of my love for the rest of my life."

There are some women who consciously believe that coyness, cunning, and game-playing are absolutely essential in their dealings with men—the only way they can hope to get what they want. But, sadly, most women who employ manipulative or indirect styles are not really aware of doing so.

"We had planned to go skiing over Valentine's Day weekend with another couple—friends of mine," recalls Michael, 25, a graduate student. "Donna was very happy and excited when I asked her to go. It would have been the first time we went away together since we've been together—about four months.

"Well, as it got closer to Valentine's Day, Donna made some very critical remarks about my friend's wife, Lori. Donna finally said I should go ahead and go without her so she could catch up on some research over the weekend. I knew she wasn't telling me the truth. We had a long talk, and what finally came out was that she was angry at me for wanting to spend a romantic weekend with the other couple. She wanted to be alone with me.

"Instead of just saying that, she had built up this real hostility for Lori. She was forcing me to choose between her and my best friends. We worked it out and had a great time skiing—all four of us—but now I find myself wondering what she *really* wants sometimes when we're having a discussion."

Patterns of communication that children learn early in their lives are wonderfully helpful if they remain relevant and appropriate to current life situations. But usually trouble results when old solutions are applied to new situations. What was appropriate with a father may be destructive with an adult lover.

It's crucial to recognize that the underlying trigger of game-playing behavior is a fear of not getting what one needs. Everyone deserves to have his basic needs met. What is at issue is not the needs themselves, but the appropriate ways to go about satisfying them. It is foolish to believe that game-playing is a viable way to accomplish that goal. It isn't. It simply alienates men and drives them away.

Hidden Dependency Needs

Royce, a talented and ambitious commercial artist, lived and worked in a downtown Los Angeles loft. She had dated many men, but never seemed to form any sort of lasting connection. Judging from her own pronouncements that she needed her independence to develop her career, it seemed as if she wasn't interested in a deep commitment to a man. At least not until she met Gary, a real estate broker who seemed the most unlikely of matches for her. In contrast to the artists and writers to whom she'd always been drawn before, Gary was stable and dependable. He was fascinated by Royce. She introduced him to an artistic, creative world he had never before known. Just six months after they met, she gave up her downtown loft and moved into his luxurious ranch home in the suburbs.

Mary had worked for IBM for the ten years since she had graduated from Vassar. It was an indication of her strong drive for independence that at age 25 she had chosen not to marry the man she was living with when she unexpectedly got pregnant. She had raised Lili, now 7, by herself and was a devoted single mother. Mary had been promoted to a managerial position when she met Tom. Their relationship was fast and intense, and Mary was thrilled. Not only did Tom care for her, but he also hit it off fabulously with her daughter. Four months after they met, Mary and Tom were married.

Sheryl was near completion of a residency in orthopedic surgery in San Francisco. She was pleased by the tough and aggressive evaluations she received from professors when she decided upon a surgical residency. In spite of the grueling hours and the demands placed upon her, she earned the respect of her fellow residents and staff surgeons. She began dating David, a staff internist at the hospital. Before David, Sheryl had assiduously avoided love affairs with doctors. "When I leave the hospital, the last things I want to talk about are cases of hospital politics." Despite these long-standing aversions, her attachment to David deepened. The week after she completed her residency she moved in with David.

What do these women have in common? They all seem independent and self-sufficient. Each established a relationship with a man who was attracted, at least in part, to these qualities. Now, let's take a look at the evolution of their relationships.

Shortly after Royce, the artist, moved in with Gary, she felt an enormous release of pressure. She began to realize how anxious she had been, how hard she had had to push herself to keep afloat financially on a free-lance basis. For the first time since leaving home she had someone with whom she could share living expenses. For the first time, too, she had a roof over her head regardless of whether she had money coming in. Royce found herself spending fewer and fewer hours in her studio in Gary's house and more and more hours puttering around the house and making fabulous gourmet dinners for Gary. She slackened her pace and stopped the energetic hustle that had been her style for so long. She spent lazy afternoons reading and even planted a vegetable garden in the backyard. She daydreamed about returning to art school and devoting herself to serious painting. But as Royce became more domesticated, Gary found himself pulling away from her. This wasn't the free-spirited and ambitious woman he wanted. He didn't see himself as a free ride or a subsidy for her art career. In short, Gary felt taken in by Royce.

Mary, the executive, had never been happier in her life. She had enjoyed her daughter and her professional success tremendously, yet had always wanted a father for Lili and a partner for herself. Tom was perfect—a wonderful father and a kind and loving husband. Soon after she and Tom married, Mary began to have a persistent and delightful fantasy about quitting work and really being a full-time mother. Before her marriage, her professional work was not an option, but a necessity. But now she felt so protected by Tom that the fantasy of quitting became a real possibility and she felt less motivated to push forward in her work. Mary discovered she was tired of the burdens and responsibilities of her job, the pressure of having to go out and perform day after day. One night after an especially passionate session of lovemaking, she shared her fantasy with Tom about quitting her work for a while. Tom was furious. He didn't want to be the sole bread-winner in his new family. Tom wanted Mary to continue to work.

Sheryl, the physician, felt as though she had been in school her whole life, and for all practical purposes, she had. She had felt comfortable in an academic environment, but was quite apprehensive about setting up her own practice. Sheryl interviewed with a number of orthopedic groups and received several attractive offers, but in each case she seemed to find at least one important ingredient missing. She found herself questioning whether she truly was interested in orthopedics; it now seemed so precise and mechanical. In contrast, living with David was easy. He encouraged her to take her time to find the right medical group to join. He understood the pressure she was under and the letdown one feels after so many years of working toward a goal. After all, he had felt it too. As the weeks went by, Sheryl found herself thinking of children, either having one herself or perhaps changing her specialty and doing a second residency in pediatrics or, better yet, pediatric orthopedics. The demands and uncertainty of private practice began to seem terrifying, and she longed for the structure and security of the familiar academic environment. She became increasingly confused, paralyzed. David's income was more than enough to support them both very comfortably. Sheryl felt confident he would endorse her plan to take some time off to find herself. But David didn't endorse her plan. Her independence and admirable competence were part of what he had cherished in her. He was disappointed and resentful that she had lost her sense of direction and ambition and now wanted to be taken care of.

How do these men react when the women they love change so radically? They are resentful. Let's explore some of the reasons why.

First of all, the men assumed that the way these women presented themselves at the beginning of the relationship was the way they really were and would continue to be. When they changed, the men felt deceived. These women had experienced how exhausting and stressful it was to be on their own, and now that they had a man to lean on, they felt they could relax. They had relinquished a significant facet of their strength and independence. From a male point of view, it was as though a hidden little girl had gradually emerged.

Actually, men feel the same urges to be dependent and to be taken care of that women do. However, most men suppress them for adaptive reasons—men have little choice but to be self-supporting. But because men have their own fantasies of dependency, they openly resent and secretly envy a woman's desire to exercise her "option" to be taken care of.

In addition, men have hidden fears concerning their own dependency needs. Traditionally, they have been taught that such needs are not masculine and are to be denied. If these needs are too apparent, it creates discomfort in most men, even shame.

Ray expresses his resentment when he describes his relationship with Dina, a hair stylist. "I was attracted to her because she was pretty, funny, athletic, and really her own person. We decided to live together for a year to find out if we got along well enough to get married and have kids. She said she wanted her own beauty salon, and we talked about saving for it and a house. Well, we got a nice apartment together, and things changed almost overnight. She had always worked three or four evenings a week before, but she stopped taking evening appointments so she could be home to cook dinner for me. Then she started complaining that she couldn't stand the owner of the salon where she worked. One day, she just quit. Now she says she wants to get married as soon as possible. Every month, I think she's going to tell me she's pregnant. Even though she's not working now, she calls me a "sexist pig" if I don't wash the dishes and help with the apartment. I think she basically wants it both ways—to be taken care of like a child and treated like a woman."

Ray had difficulty adjusting to Dina's need for a liberated man while she still had the freedom to choose whichever role she desired. As Ray describes his feelings, "It seems as if she's got the best of both worlds, and I'm stuck with the worst."

There is certainly nothing wrong with wanting to lean on someone—that's what lovers, families, and close friends are for. And, of course, most men today understand that career women must take time off in order to bear children and begin a family. But when these needs are hidden and overpowering and then suddenly emerge as a surprise in a relationship, they can create serious problems.

Many women, particularly in recent years, have learned to conceal dependency needs from themselves and others. They think of themselves as self-sufficient and confident. They look for men who not only accept but also value and appreciate their autonomy. These women are often as shocked as their men when their "strong woman" facade crumbles. Naively, the newly revealed little girl in these women assumes the "perfect" man they chose naturally will be able to handle her new set of needs and emotions. After all, a "real man" shouldn't resent dependency. But most often, even the "real man" does. He fell in love with an independent woman and didn't realize that a little girl went along in the bargain.

Fortunately, there are early warning signs of such hidden dependency needs. Penelope Russianoff's *Why Do I Think I'm Nothing Without a Man?* and Colette Dowling's *The Cinderella Complex* explore these issues with fascinating insight. One obvious early warning sign is when dreams of marriage are linked with thoughts of total security, even when a woman is aware intellectually that marriage is not an absolute protection blanket from life's insecurities and problems.

Dependency needs hide behind another disguise, the excessive compulsion to control a relationship. Jessica, a 26-year-old department store buyer, relates, "Before Pete, I never had trouble being warm and affectionate with men. But with him, I felt this terrible anxiety. I had to push him and test him and make him show that he loved me more than I loved him, make him give while I held back and acted like a real bitch. I was in constant terror that he would get the upper hand and reject me."

By not giving fully of her love, not opening up emotionally, Jessica did not have to face or reveal to Pete her powerful, hidden need for him. When we allow ourselves to become soft and vulnerable, our dependency needs shoot right to the surface.

Many women may find themselves suddenly longing to walk away from hard-earned careers soon after they connect deeply with a man who offers economic security. They may fantasize about going back to school or developing their creative talents. What many women fail to realize is that many men would like to do the same things. For the most part, however, men have to moonlight creative expression. For men who lack private fortunes, doing something "meaningful" (read: low or no pay) or continuing their education has to be accommodated around a full-time work schedule. Not surprisingly, the woman who wants to quit work to fulfill herself can spark deep resentment in the man who not only can't allow himself the same luxury, but also is expected to support the endeavor.

Women can't make radical changes in their goals and attitudes and expect men to automatically support them. Changes in expectations and life plans must evolve slowly and mutually.

The Hunger for Love

Very young children are connected to their parents by an invisible umbilical cord of appropriate, healthy dependency. A child's love is primarily a selfish and one-sided experience. It isn't until the process of socialization gradually takes hold that children learn concern and sensitivity for others and begin to experience the magical rewards of giving love as well as receiving it.

Childhood experiences with love vary tremendously. Some of us were fortunate in being made to feel valued and loved by our parents. But many of us were left with an incomplete experience of love. The scars of this early damage to one's sense of lovability and personal value may lead to a desperation which in adulthood acts as a barrier to love. Instead of inviting the compassion and understanding we deserve from others, these old wounds frequently have the effect of actually putting others off.

It's a sad paradox that women who most need love often have the least chance of finding it, especially when they are unaware of the signals of desperation they send that may alienate men. They don't necessarily deny to themselves that they have strong needs, but they are unaware of the ways these needs are communicated to men.

A woman's desperation may be experienced by men as an empty hole, a deep, dark, bottomless pit. It terrifies them. Desperation in no way communicates the capacity to *give* love; it shouts only the fierce need to *be* loved. Desperation is an unspoken hunger that reveals itself as surely as if a woman had a message tattooed on her forehead: "Love me! Please love me!"

There is something very fundamental that women need to understand about men. Even the most confident and secure of our male patients report that part of what they look for in a relationship are the qualities of nurturance, warmth, and sensitivity they experienced from their mothers when they were young. Men will never casually inform a woman of this, but it is true nonetheless. Even today, when it's supposedly acceptable for men to acknowledge these "softer" needs, they are reluctant to appear "weak" in so doing. Although there are still men for whom the need to feel warm and close is to some degree denied, the maternal component most men search for in women is enormously important. When it's absent, men may conclude that a woman is too self-absorbed or desperate. Why? Because men interpret its absence in a woman as reflecting a need to take, not a capacity to give.

How is desperation transmited? Men are sensitive to certain extremely subtle clues. Men's radar for desperation begins flashing when women give importance to a relationship long before it has a chance to really develop. They pick up on expectations that are too quick, too intense, too demanding. They sense a woman's hunger when expressions of affection and endearment come too soon, or when "I love you" has a plaintive question mark tacked on the end—an indirect request to be reassured. A desperate woman demands a commitment before the relationship seed has taken root. Desperation doesn't believe that left to grow at its own magical pace, love will blossom. Desperation poisons a relationship long before romance can even get started.

The woman who denies her hunger for love frequently is baffled when men abruptly turn off to her. Recalling their encounter, she can find nothing she said or did—intentionally—that would explain why he didn't phone again.

Debbie is a 37-year-old engineer. Abandoned by alcoholic parents when she was 5, she was raised by a harshly religious grandmother. Debbie has never married, nor has she ever lived with a man. She is active in several singles' groups, but she's rarely asked for a second date. Debbie describes her situation: "I've really only had three boyfriends in my whole life, and the longest relationship lasted only one year. It's not as if I'm looking for the moon—just a nice, decent guy. I'd like to have at least one child, and I know my time is running out. I'm a good listener, I'm as nice as I can be on dates and try to act confident, casual, and fun, but I keep scaring them away. Sure I'm feeling desperate—wouldn't you be?"

Debbie not only sounds nice, she *is* nice. Her only problem is that her lack of success in making a connection with a man has created a hungry edge, communicating what has verged upon panic over not finding someone to love her. No matter how she tries to hide it, the fear shows and men unfortunately find it frightening rather than appealing.

Even though such women are often perfectly capable of loving and being loved by men, men tend to recoil from them. Repeated rejections reinforce deep-seated feelings of unlovability and serve only to intensify the desperation and its signals to men.

Ron, an insurance adjuster, talks about the reactions he had to Ginny, a co-worker he dated briefly. "I don't know exactly what turned me off to her. I really liked her. Ginny is friendly and outgoing and attractive. I think maybe it's that she tries a little too hard. When we went out a few times, to the movies or for dinner, she acted so grateful. She kept asking if she was dressed right and really pushed me into bed with her the second date. Now, when I see her coming, I find myself kind of hunching my shoulders and physically recoiling, and all she's doing is being friendly!"

Although Ron may not fully understand his reaction to Ginny, he is recoiling from her intense emotional needs. Women who come across as starving for love scare the hell out of men. And the longer such women are deprived of love, the hungrier they get. If these women weren't so desperate, men would be more readily inclined to love them. It may sound as if we are saying, "Don't be so hungry!" to a starving person. That's pretty ludicrous, and we don't mean that. Desperation is a symptom of low self-esteem and pessimism about one's lovability. The only lasting solution is for a woman to develop trust in her own worthiness, and to transform her self-image so that she can perceive herself as a person worthy of being loved. The desperate woman looks to others to validate her worth. She foolishly thinks that the "right" man will be the solution to her feelings of incompleteness. Not only is the right man not a solution, but when this woman acts according to these feelings she's bound to drive men away.

The first step for women in dealing with desperation is recognizing and accepting that their hunger may be out of control, then learning to contain it—not deny or suppress it, but contain it. The key to doing this is to become more self-confident and allow relationships to unfold gradually and mutually instead of rushing commitment.

The containment of emotional hunger is not an easy task. It requires continued faith that success, and thus enhanced self-esteem, will certainly follow—and it does. In fact, the very decision to look elsewhere for ways of bolstering one's confidence acts to contain and diminish desperation.

Dependency needs get both women and men into trouble, primarily when they attempt to deny them. It is then that they manifest themselves as self-defeating and inappropriate behavior. As a relationship deepens, needs and insecurities should be talked about and healthily satisfied through an easy give-and-take with men.

It is true that some men do thrive on a woman's dependency on them—to be needed so fiercely bolsters their own self-image. In fact, such men feel comfortable only when they are in this position of the rescuing knight. The dark side of this man is petty tyranny. Beware! He is likely to sabotage and thwart any attempt on a woman's part to become more independent—often with such subtlety and finesse she may be barely aware he's doing it.

*   *   *

We believe that women are realizing that
they cannot capture what they had, or wish
they had had, with their fathers. They are
assuming responsibility for their own self-worth
and sense of completion. By mastering such
feelings independent of their relationships with
men, women are able to engage in the sort of
mutually nurturing, yet individually self-sufficient partnership that is the emerging para-
digm for lasting and successful relationships.

CHAPTER FOUR

How Men Respond to Power in Women

In order to clearly understand men and how they view women, it's important to know something about the images, fears, and wishes that forge the unconscious male psyche. We believe that women often feel they know men when in fact they are often quite unaware of the deeper forces that shape male behavior. This understanding is critical to making smart choices with men.

Since the first stirring of civilization, men have been in awe of women's capacity to give life. Probably after a good deal of trial and error, men hit upon a masterful tactic. They simply hid the awesome dimensions of their need and deceived women into believing it was really they who needed men more. This strategy served a number of purposes. Men could feel needed by women, ignore some of their own dependency needs, and thus feel stronger and more in control. Whenever men or women feel frightened, they create myths to assuage their anxiety. So men created myths about women. If you examine mythology and fables about women throughout history and look beneath the thin veneer of postured superiority, you will see male envy and fear. The variety of myths men have created about women and their power is truly staggering. They range from woman as earth mother to woman as insatiable whore. There are fables about wild and uncontrollable women whose capacity for passion was far superior to any man's. In many, many cultures the woman has been depicted as an enchantress—the seductress who leads men astray. In the Bible, we see Eve's feminine wiles lead Adam into temptation. In Greek mythology, the most mysterious and fearsome powers were those possessed by the Sirens; so powerful were these creatures they could lure men to their deaths.

During the Middle Ages and with the rise of Christianity, purity and virginity became the new virtues that women were supposed to uphold. This was not really an attempt to model women after the Virgin Mother, but a clever device designed by men to ensure that women were faithful to their mates.

Perhaps you are saying to yourself, "Come on, we don't live that way anymore." Even though we are more sophisticated about the nature of men and women and know a lot more than our ancestors did, our basic instincts, our deep unconscious psychology, have not changed all that much. Just as the earliest-known works of art, created by men, were fertility symbols, our basic perception of the opposite sex is rooted in the primordial ooze of early civilization—the influences may be largely unconscious, but they're there and affect us all.

The All-Powerful Mother

Let's take a look at the early-childhood experience of men to see how fear and envy begin. And remember, as we go along, that many of these feelings are alive and well in men, even as adults.

From the first moments of their existence, men are dependent upon women. It is the mother who traditionally recognizes and satisfies her son's every need. She is the one who nurses him, comforts him, and is attentive to the subtlest shifts in his mood and physical well-being. The father is often a mysterious and inconsistent figure. Traditionally, he has been the breadwinner and consequently has had less time to spend with his children. So when a child falls, for example, the cry for help is for "Mommy" rather than "Daddy."

Although in recent years fathers have begun taking a much more active parenting role, most adult males were surrounded by women during childhood—their mothers, their friends' mothers, and female teachers. This concentrated exposure to women combined with fathers' working is one reason why men are said to be overly "feminized" at an early age.

A mother has a powerful and central role in a boy's life. He is bonded to her, yet he eventually must learn to disengage from his mother in order to develop and define himself as a boy and, ultimately, as a man. If boys fail to make this separation, they can become confused and insecure in their sexual identity.

Boys are taught to feel a threat or danger in staying too close to their mothers because such initially pleasant feelings of closeness and dependency ultimately lead to fears of weakness, becoming a "sissy" or a "momma's boy." Fathers frequently make deprecating comments to their sons about their closeness to and need for their mothers. And peers make it clear very quickly that dependency on one's mother can be expressed openly only at the expense of derision and perhaps ostracism from friends. Yet even grown men carry within them a yearning to embrace and to be embraced by that all-loving mother figure—a yearning which often finds expression during times of great danger, need, or even celebration. A poignant example of the depth of this yearning can be seen in men who almost reflexively cry out "Mother!" when wounded on the battlefield. Even during bouts of minor illness, many men revert to babyhood. They do this for two reasons. First, illness brings to the surface old, familiar memories of being taken care of by a concerned, attentive, loving mother. Second, illness can provide men with a justification for indulging their yearning to be mothered. They can let down their guard and allow themselves to be fussed over without feeling ashamed of their enjoyment of being babied.

In adulthood, when men are drawn to intimate attachments with women, they experience both pleasure and fear—the pleasure of being nurtured by a woman and fear that these deeply ingrained feelings of helplessness and dependency will overwhelm them.

Rick, a 36-year-old landscape artist, says, "Every time I let myself fall in love I end up with this sick, scary feeling inside. I guess I forget how needy I can be. At first, I feel terrific with her, but after a while I start making her the center of my life. When she leaves for work in the morning, I don't want to let her go. I let myself get so connected to her that I end up feeling pretty weak. Eventually, I find myself backing away. I don't want to let any woman have that kind of power over me."

Rick's unresolved feelings toward his mother unfortunately influence his relationships with women. He is an example of the man who repeatedly runs from commitment. He had an overprotective and domineering mother he was close to, perhaps too close. The intensity of his need for a woman creates an equally intense fear of being enveloped by her, and being weakened by his own need for her.

To say that men are afraid of intimacy is to miss the point. We believe men do want intimacy. But men are unsure of how to deal with the feelings of helplessness that accompany letting their guard down and allowing themselves to need a woman. They are afraid that the woman will not be as warm and loving as their mother, or as they wished their mother might have been. We're not implying that all men seek out surrogate mothers, but as we noted in the previous chapter, most men do watch for signs of warm maternal qualities in a woman. The truth is that most men don't want to be tough all the time, and they form the strongest connections with women who understand and accept this, who feel comfortable enough with their own nurturing abilities to give to a man when the need arises. What we are saying is that ultimately for even short but sweet periods of time, men would like to and may need to make contact with the soft and maternal part of a woman—not to remain there forever, but rather to confirm its existence and the acceptability of their availing themselves of its gift.

We believe that women who blind themselves to these needs in men are making a terribly foolish choice. Men do pay attention to a woman's maternal potential—a lot of attention. And caution flags come up if they don't see evidence of that promise in a woman. Mark, a 39-year-old loan officer, describes what he is looking for in a relationship: "At this point in my life I'm aware that I need a lot of different things in a woman. I really like a woman to be independent and strong, but as much as I like that, I know it's also important to find her to be soft and compassionate, sort of mothering when I need it. I'm not necessarily proud of it, but I know I need to feel this security before I can say 'I love you' to a woman."

Mothers have a powerful impact on their sons, which influences their adult relationships with women. A woman can't change these influences, but she *can* learn to understand them.

The New Impotency

With the sexual revolution, women recognized the right to express their sexual needs and desires openly and freely; men lost their long-held sexual control over women. But as beneficial as the sexual revolution has been for both women and men, it is unfortunately true that, in recent years, men's performance anxiety has greatly increased. Called the "new impotency," it can be so severe that some men completely withdraw from sexual contacts.

Although many men profess to enjoy a more sexually aggressive woman, in fact there are doubts and fears that may surface in the man regarding his ability as a lover. It is vitally important for smart women to recognize and be sensitive to these feelings.

The women's movement encouraged men to be less rigidly macho and more expressive of their feelings. But in so doing, men opened up a Pandora's box of anxieties. Suppression of their sensitivity protected men from this now direct experience of certain fears.

Take Phil's revelation in group therapy, for example. One evening, he sarcastically noted his progress in learning to be more open with his feelings.

"I'm closer to more women, I'm learning to let them in and get to know me, but now the bad news—I'm becoming a lousy lover, especially with aggressive women. When a woman approaches me directly, I shrivel up and run like hell!" Let's hope that men are just in a transition stage—but there are many Phils out there now, reconciling new and old attitudes about lovemaking.

Men have a strong need to maintain their sexual self-esteem. Sometimes women have difficulty making sense of the often subtle and complex nature of male sexuality, and the puzzling ways male sexual-performance anxiety crops up in relationships.

For men, the importance of sexual activity often involves what it "means" rather than what it feels like. Whereas women primarily relate to their sexual experience in terms of direct emotional intimacy and sensual pleasure, sexual activity for men also has an important symbolic component involving accomplishment and conquest. Men enjoy making love in the physical sense, certainly, but it has another important meaning for them—validation of masculinity or manhood. To feel humiliated in the sexual arena is to suffer the greatest anguish that most men can experience, for often their very identity hinges upon sexual performance.

As a result of these anxieties, most men harbor a fantasy wish for a "steel phallus," the hard and instant erection—both symbolically and literally. There is a desire to be strong, tough, to spring into action, to feel potent. Just as some men are afraid to be soft outside of bed, they are even more frightened of being soft in bed!

If a man is nervous during a sexual encounter, adrenaline-like substances are released which affect the functioning of his autonomic nervous system. This, in turn, constricts his blood vessels. This constriction prevents the flow of blood to the penis, making it difficult to get or maintain an erection. In other words, his anxiety about his performance is a self-fulfilling prophecy.

The fear of softness is threatening to men because it evokes a primitive sense of helplessness. Men feel they must be "hard" and stay "hard" to be successful. Not to do so is to experience failure and shame.

How do men relate to their sexual partner when these distressing events occur? In contrast to the powerful and reassuring fantasy of the steel phallus, at these times men experience unfocused fears often characterized as castration anxieties. When we use the term "castration anxiety," what we mean is the male fear of opening up and entrusting himself to a woman. To sexually let go with a woman is to yield to her. As Carol Gilligan has noted, men fear entrapment and engulfment, a feeling of helplessness. Of course, the man doesn't fear actual castration, but he does fear losing something—his strength. He is most exposed and vulnerable to the woman when he fears or actually experiences lapses in potency, for they are intimately linked with his sense of strength and masculinity.

Mike is a single man in his mid-thirties. He is successful in his work, confident and self-assured with women. Nevertheless, he has nagging fears about performance. "There's always that moment in bed, no matter how lusty I feel, when I wonder whether my turned-on feelings are going to flow into my penis. It's like a little nagging doubt in my head. Thank God, I don't pay attention to it very often."

Often in therapy with couples we encounter a man who insists that he wants his partner to initiate sex more often, but when she does, trouble frequently ensues. Suddenly, he feels unprepared, taken off-guard. He may be tired or preoccupied with career concerns. He may not be able to achieve an erection. He often realizes that what he wanted was not that his partner be more aggressive, but rather more direct and expressive of her desire for him. Whatever men say, most of them still like to control the timing and frequency of lovemaking.

In sustained relationships, some men find they don't know how to tell a partner they are not in the mood for sex. They don't realize it is perfectly normal to feel this way at times, for many of them have been programmed to think the man should "always be ready." One maladaptive but all too common way men have learned to handle this feeling is to provoke fights to obscure their real desire to avoid sexual activity.

Linda found her sex life with Marc seemed to have lost its fire and was slowly dwindling to nothing. After several frustrating months, they sought counseling. Marc protested they weren't making love because they fought too much at night. After some exploration, we unearthed the fact that Marc went out of his way to inject complaints into their talk just as they were going to bed. Starting World War III made lovemaking out of the question. Over a period of time, Marc was helped to understand how nervous he was about their sexual relationship and how that apprehension prompted him to look for ways to avoid sex and, in doing so, to reduce his anxiety about it.

Because of their performance concerns, when men say they want a woman who is sexually aggressive, what they usually mean is that they want a woman who will be exquisitely responsive and passionate when they make known their desire to make love. We are not implying that this is the way it should be or that women shouldn't be aggressive sexually. Rather, we are pointing out that some men are intimidated by women who are sexually aggressive, a factor women should be aware of and then make whatever decisions they feel comfortable with.

Not only are men anxious about their ability to get erections, but they are also unnerved about the female orgasm. It wasn't all that long ago that the female orgasm was a mystery, poorly understood by either men or women. As the facts of the female orgasm were revealed, men found they had a new fascination and, unfortunately, a new worry.

Whereas in the past men didn't feel guilty when a woman failed to reach orgasm, now they realize that any woman can climax, provided she and her lover have the requisite patience, interest, and skills. Women now expect more time and sensitivity from their lovers, and rightfully so.

Unfortunately, however, many men see the sensitivity and patience required of them in foreplay as work. And if a man feels it is an effort, the woman senses it. Then he notices her noticing his discomfort and they both become uncomfortable. Eventually, each becomes exhausted. The two performance anxieties, hers and his, feed each other.

Phil had expressed his fears this way: "I'm

seeing a woman whom I really care a lot about. The sex was great at first. But now it is changing. Usually, I come first, and then I try to satisfy her. I want to. I'm really into it. But after a while, I get tired and less excited. Then she starts to feel guilty and tries too hard herself, and then she finally gets turned off."

In order to remove some of the pressure to perform, many men try to have the woman reach orgasm first. But in the process, men often lose some of their own arousal. Any hint of their softening triggers concern and may put a damper on the experience. When a man varies in the degree of his arousal, it is usually reflected in the quality of his erection. This is why many men are uncomfortable with the normal waxing and waning of arousal during lovemaking. Only through acceptance of these natural rhythms of arousal can men learn to relax, be less hurried, and participate in satisfying lovemaking. Fortunately, men seem to be learning this lesson. As one man expressed it, "I always had a thought in the back of my mind that I might get soft, so I'd rush lovemaking. Now I take it all in stride; whatever happens is okay. I can relax, and if I lose my erection, I know I'll eventually find it again!"

To summarize, the need to perform sexually is at the core of some men's fear and defensiveness toward women who are sexually assertive, and women need to understand this to deal sensitively and successfully with men. Many women have told us, for example, that when they have spent a wonderful evening and night together for the first time with a man, sometimes he never calls again. It may be that he feels he can't live up to his first peak performance. The self-imposed pressure to "live up to" some sexual standard causes many men to disappear, unfortunately leaving many women wondering what they did wrong. Or perhaps both the woman and the man were nervous, and the sex was not spectacular. Again, the woman may not hear from the man. Men have greater difficulty than do women in accepting that sexual discomfort is normal in the beginning. Such a man is afraid there will be a repeat of his shyness and awkwardness.

If we all just learned to relax, have fun, and enjoy giving pleasure to someone about whom we care, there would be fewer problems. But too frequently, we fall prey to the notion that our self-worth is dependent, to a significant degree, on our skills as sexual partners.

The Passive-Aggressive Response

Some men's solution to fears of strength and power in woman is to take a passive role. Instead of dealing with their anxiety, such men totally succumb to the wish to be taken care of by "Mommy," the powerful female who will nurture them. As we've pointed out, both men and women have desires to be "taken care of," but some men choose this path exclusively. The problem is that the fear is still present in these men, except now it is hidden.

Men who, though not outwardly passive, invariably gravitate toward the stronger woman are in psychological terms "oral." They are insatiable in their need to be nurtured and often supplement this need through alcohol or drugs. These men allow themselves to be taken care of by a "Florence Nightingale" type, the woman who becomes a savior. Unfortunately, this woman gets taken in, feels he is only temporarily down on his luck, and fantasizes that he'll soon regain his strength through her caring and compassion.

Bob is a sporadically employed salesman who is energetic when motivated, but soon loses interest in his job and either quits or gets fired. The truth is, he enjoys not working. There's more time to ski, chase women, drink, do drugs, and generally "party down." Michelle fell for Bob right away, even though he didn't hide his heavy drinking from her. She saw how pleasure-oriented and basically non-serious he was about his life, his work, and their relationship, but she believed he had potential.

She was determined to "save" him. Eventually, Bob moved in with Michelle and revealed more of his underlying neediness. She became a mother or big sister to him. Her friends warned her Bob would never become the responsible husband she said she wanted, but Bob's problems all seemed temporary to Michelle. She insisted he would get back on his feet. Instead, Bob got worse, to the point where he was drinking heavily for days at a time and becoming more and more irritable and irrational. Michelle finally threw him out. It was only after she had suffered considerable abuse that Michelle gave up and finally saw that Bob's problems were more than she could either handle or change.

The passive male is frequently a sensitive soul who has a great deal of raw ability and potential, but because of his passivity he fails to make his mark in the world. Again, there are women who will be inexorably drawn to this sensitivity. But rather than accepting his basic nature, many of these women want to be "good" mothers and help him realize his potential by encouraging him to release his energy and power. This type of man often seems appreciative and usually allows himself to go along with the program.

Unfortunately, some of these men are not merely passive, but passive-aggressive. What this means is that beneath their passive facade they are angrily digging in their heels. They really don't want to be more assertive, and they will sabotage any attempts to change them. Eventually, they will drive these women crazy just the way they may have wanted to rebel against their mothers.

Jimmy, 27, started his own accounting business right out of college. But somehow he just couldn't seem to make a go of it. He lacked the initiative and confidence to go out and get new clients. When he got depressed he would come home early, get into bed, and read. His girlfriend, Cindy, had her own financial consulting business. By contrast, she was very enterprising and successful. Upon her urging, they entered couples therapy, in which at one point she declared that she just wanted to help him "learn to be more aggressive and drum up business." He sat smiling and nodding as though he had the same goal, but he clearly didn't. Throughout Jim's life he had been with powerful women who tried to help him. While outwardly compliant, he was secretly enraged that they couldn't accept him as he was. Cindy finally realized that she wasn't accepting his basic passivity and if she truly wanted him, she had to change her expectations. She eventually admitted to herself that she actually was more comfortable and secure being the stronger one in the relationship.

Not all relationship crises are resolved so neatly, especially when they involve the passive male with the more assertive woman. Most passive men come to accept themselves. But the women they marry often have foolish and naive beliefs about the essential nature of their men. For these women, the task is to realize they chose such a man not because of his potential strength, but because they actually may feel more secure in a dominant role. Acting as the helpmate can be a potent way for a woman to both maintain a sense of control and validate herself as a concerned and involved partner.

Sometimes, however, a seriously passive man can come to envy and resent a woman. Nan, a woman in her late forties, has been divorced for three years. Her ex-husband was fascinating because of his sensitive and creative nature but was not successful in any worldly way. It's only been recently that Nan realized how he resented her success in the entertainment industry and covertly sniped and clawed at her each time she had a success. Even though he did nothing to focus his own energy toward specific achievement, he resented Nan's ability to do so even though she was generous in offering him help, suggestions, and encouragement. She was sad about this rather than angry, for she also realized that he was probably unaware of the deep fury he held inside.

It's critical for strong women to be sure of their mate's genuine support and unthreatened appreciation. In healthy relationships, mates tend to take turns parenting each other when needed. A woman must guard against falling into the trap of being endlessly maternal with a man. Boys resent their mothers when the dependency goes on too long, and they leave them and find girlfriends!

The Fear Of Angry Women

One of the effects of the women's liberation movement was anger and outrage on the part of women. Any group that has been held down tends to erupt when the shackles are released. And that is exactly what happened.

Rape was a central issue. Women were furious that this act of degradation and violation had been treated so lightly not only in the courts but also in the minds of men. Rape became a metaphor, a general symbol of the manner in which women had been taken advantage of and oppressed by men for centuries.

Another vital issue was the way women were, and unfortunately continue to be, depreciated and exploited in the work force. Such factors as unequal pay and sexual discrimination in the workplace were finally given serious consideration. The injustices were obvious and well documented, yet attempts to right these wrongs are still slow in coming.

The male response to these outrages was complex. Some men were blind and insensitive to issues of inequality and needed to be educated even to become aware of them. In their hearts and private thoughts, though, many men came to see that injustices and inequalities had existed. They realized that the core tenets of feminism were well-taken and just. But men were also alarmed by the anger they saw erupting from women even as they attempted to become more sensitive to these issues.

In our discussion here, we do mean *anger*, not assertion. Assertion is a decisive and clear pattern of affirmative behavior, while anger is an intense negative emotion. Unfortunately, assertion and anger sometimes become confused. This confusion arises in part because assertive behavior can be fueled by old feelings of anger or resentment, making it difficult for both men and women to clearly see assertive behavior as separate from anger.

We're not suggesting that women be passive or keep justified anger under wraps. We're merely describing the impact of anger and noting that sometimes the line between assertion and anger gets blurred, for example, in the workplace. Melinda is a marketing manager for a large manufacturing company. She's bright, ambitious, and assertive. When she was new on the job, her male associates joked among themselves that she was "out-machoing them." After some time, these men felt progressively more uncomfortable with her. Her reaction was to become even tougher, and as she did, they withdrew. The chip on her shoulder became a self-fulfilling prophecy: The harder and more competitive she became, the more alienated the men were. What she failed to realize was that they would have reacted in the same manner if she had been a man.

In an interview, Jane Evans, executive vice-president of General Mills Corporation, one of the highest-ranking female executives in the U.S., outlined the task for women in the corporate world. She suggests women need "wit, warmth, and a sense of humor" and that they be "toughminded, not hardhearted" in order for men to learn to be comfortable with them. In Chapter Twelve, we will explore the ways in which this balance of strength and softness can be realized.

The confusion between anger and assertion is most damaging to women when it happens in love relationships. Just as men do, some women feel powerful when they express anger. But it can be detrimental to achieving intimacy. Angry women frighten men. It's that simple. Because of the deep, nurturing connection men crave, anger is even more frightening coming from a woman than from another man. It never feels good to be on the receiving end of anger. So a lot of men turn tail and run from angry women.

Rhonda, a 33-year-old actress, is absolutely convinced that her cynical and bitter attitudes toward men and relationships are well disguised. She is wrong. She possesses a razor-sharp and irreverent sense of humor and carves away at men's frailties with the skill of a surgeon. At first, men are so taken with her beauty and wit that they don't realize she actually means the hostile things she says; they are couched in such hilarious terms that most men fall on the floor with laughter.

Curt, a 39-year-old internist, was captivated by Rhonda, who so freely said and did whatever she wanted, seemingly effortlessly. Curt was used to women in his life making the accommodations to his demanding schedule and life-style. Not so with Rhonda, whose pace was even busier than his own. Curt made the adjustments, went to her screenings, and spent time with her friends. He saw her according to her availability, which frequently changed capriciously even though he had gone to great lengths to make sure someone was on call for him. Times when they were with each other were typically spent in the company of her close women friends. Out of earshot of Curt, she joked that she was now "working a doctor." Rhonda told Curt she didn't want to meet his friends because doctors—except for him, of course—were too boring. And although Rhonda indicated that she liked and respected Curt, she also was quick to disparage men in general at every opportunity.

One evening, at a Hollywood dinner party, everyone including Rhonda was involved in a heated debate about a new director. Curt had left the room, and when he returned, he didn't know who they were discussing. He politely asked who this person was. Rhonda turned to him. "Honey, don't you try to keep up with us—this is movie talk." Curt, burning with humiliation, didn't speak for the rest of the evening. He dropped Rhonda off at her house and never called her again.

"I guess I always felt off-guard with her," he said in session. "I guess I liked it in the beginning. She had this amazing way of throwing out hostile barbs cleverly and humorously, and she expected me not to notice I was bleeding.

She certainly never expected me to point out how angry she was."

It is important for both women and men to recognize that we all carry around painful emotions from the past. We've all been hurt, disappointed, and embittered by events in our lives. And anytime we encounter a new person or situation that even unconsciously reminds us of an old wound, we may react with guardedness, anger, or bitterness. It's important to learn to discriminate between situations where that anger is appropriate and those where it really isn't deserved. If a man warrants a woman's anger, she should let him have it. We don't mean to suggest that she should ever stifle or suppress justified rage. But if he is merely a convenient target for old, unrelated resentments, such feelings are better contained. Their expression may hurt and alienate the man forever.

CHAPTER FIVE

How Exciting Men Can Make Women Miserable

That rat! Every time I start to believe he really does care about me, he stands me up or does something equally rotten. Everything happens his way, on his terms. I know I should tell him to get lost, but I can't. Being with him makes me feel alive in a way I've never felt before."

Variations on these feelings usually come from women who are embarrassed even to admit them. They often have difficulty figuring out why they ever allowed themselves to get involved in these painful relationships in the first place. They feel victimized, and yet they consistently seek out men who make them unhappy.

Nobody wants to be miserable, right? Wrong! Misery and anguish can feel delicious, while the predictability of steady, supportive love can get tiresome.

Some women crave that which ultimately may prove self-defeating but which at the time feels novel, dangerous, and compelling. Romance can be exquisitely painful. It has always been linked with the powerful feelings of longing and sadness. These emotions have origins as deep and as primitive as a child's first emotional connection. Experiences of need, love, fulfillment, and wishes in a relationship all involve a state of tension or uncertainty. Such feelings or tensions are strong and exciting, however frightening they may seem. They set our internal alarm systems jangling. They signify life, arousal, and intensity!

Women today are in a state of transition. They're caught between the sometimes illusory safety of traditional roles on the one hand and the challenge to realize their potential outside those roles on the other. Women are reexamining and redefining their ideas about themselves as well as their relationships with men. They are expecting and demanding greater sensitivity on the part of men and are looking for men strong and flexible enough to be comfortable with the changes they are trying to make.

So why the fascination with the "wrong men"

and the lack of interest in the "nice" ones? The good, stable provider who works excessively and has little understanding of the growing spectrum of a woman's needs and interests is no longer satisfying. Neither are many women enamored of the sensitive, poetic type of man, because his frequent lack of drive and aggressiveness erodes their confidence in his potential for achievement, protection, and providing a good income.

Today, women are looking for men who are a rare hybrid of glamour, excitement, and power combined with sensitivity, warmth, and protectiveness. They are looking for nothing short of perfection. What is unfortunate is that some women actually believe they will find it. Casting aside genuinely nice men who fall short of such perfection, these women propel themselves instead toward the challenge and the sweet promise offered in the mysterious relationship.

Who Is the Nice Guy?

Many women react to the term "nice" as if it meant "nerd." They might say, "Oh, you mean that jerky kind of guy who keeps telling you how beautiful you are and immediately wants to spend twenty-four hours a day with you?"

Or they may respond to "nice" as a trait to distrust. As one woman put it, "He seemed so considerate, honest, and honorable. So I let down my defenses. I was warmer and more receptive than I'd been with a guy in a long time. He stayed the night and I felt wonderfully free in letting him know I cared. In the morning he said he would call that same evening. It never occurred to me he wouldn't, since he'd been in such hot pursuit. But he didn't. After several days, I called him, and he launched into some phony story in that high voice men get when they lie. I guess he could be nice and solicitous until he captured me."

It's clear that there are wide differences in women's reactions to what's "nice" in men. What we mean by "nice" encompasses honesty, sensitivity, trust, strength, and the capacity to love. All that sounds great, right? So why then don't women naturally gravitate toward these men and value those attributes?

Let's take a closer look at what these men are like. There are basically two types of nice men, those who genuinely are nice and those who pretend to be. One has natural qualities of giving while the other is fearful and dons a mask of niceness to protect himself. Many women are confused by the two.

Sometimes Nice Is Weak

Men have gone through many changes in recent decades. During the 1950s, it was acceptable for men to be insensitive, cut off from their feelings and comfortably robotlike and macho in their aspirations. While the Beat Generation was praising the virtues of experimentation and sexual adventure, most American men read *Playboy* instead. It was the era of the crewcut corporation man who wore button-down shirts and chinos, watched a lot of Sunday football on TV, and worried about communism. And while men no doubt felt burdened by the pressures of being the breadwinner, they rarely considered the possibility of their wives' also having steady careers.

The 1960s and early 1970s were a time when men let their hair down, both literally and figuratively. Joni Mitchell was singing "I Am Golden," and everyone was reading Erich Fromm's *The Art of Loving.* Tired of clanking around in their armor, men began to discover and embrace the more suppressed, vulnerable, emotional, "feminine" aspects of their personalities.

In the late 1960s, many women were increasingly discontented with the constraints of rigid gender stereotypes. They were actively experimenting with sexual freedom and becoming more assertive. Such revolutionary changes led men to channel their fear and mistrust of this new woman into an identification with her. Thus their fears were masked by a superficial understanding of and empathy toward women.

This masked "nice guy" is truly a wolf in sheep's clothing. He is often hard to detect at first, as he is quite skilled at maintaining his disguise. But if one looks closely he can easily be identified by three basic traits. First, this "nice guy" never really gets angry—at least not at first. Second, he is wonderfully sensitive and understanding—again, for a time. And third, he is highly motivated to be supportive and helpful provided the woman expresses, early and often, her gratitude and appreciation, and also spends all her free time with him.

But, in fact, this "nice guy" lacks confidence in himself and is torn between his compelling need for women and his secret fear of them. So compelling is his need for women that he identifies with their struggles in order to confirm his sensitivity and secure their trust. Watch out! This same "nice guy" can be counted on to subtly sabotage the woman as soon as he senses that she is becoming too strong or independent.

Jim is one such "nice guy." He's been hurt in the past by a number of failed relationships. He has hidden his scars well, however, and outwardly doesn't seem to bear any grudges. He's bright, sensitive, but a bit controlled, especially on the first date. He tends to express humanitarian concerns, seemingly discusses women's issues in a positive way, and is somewhat put off by loud and aggressive people. His last girlfriend was an artist who was too "flaky" for him, or so he says. He becomes silent during a fight and tends to pout. He says he's drawn toward strong women because he likes their "spirit." But the more "alive" the woman, the more likely is he to withdraw, or to become subtly critical or suppressive of her. Ultimately a man like Jim gives only to get.

Obviously, this "nice guy" is better avoided. Rather than being genuinely supportive, this man tends to drain a woman, and when her frustration mounts, he confuses her all the more by denying the validity of her perceptions about him. A smart woman frequently will test this kind of man by pushing him to the point where any other man would get angry. If he doesn't, she secretly knows his understanding demeanor is a fake—a mask over his fear. Unfortunately, however, some women distrust their own perceptions and may feel guilty or bad for being so "suspicious." In general, nice guys who stir up mixed feelings are trouble. His niceness is probably a facade.

When Nice Looks Weak but Isn't

As noticed previously, while men have been taught to deny or at least attempt to ignore dependency needs, women traditionally have been taught to accept them and to look for their expression and satisfaction in relationships.

Jenny, a 33-year-old sixth-grade teacher, wanted to break off a relationship she'd been having with Fred, another teacher at her school. Although Fred was intelligent, sensitive, and consistent in his interest in and caring for her, Jenny was taken aback when he confessed to feeling insecure about their relationship, fearful that she would tire of him and reject him.

Even though it was difficult and embarrassing for her to admit, Jenny felt vaguely uncomfortable with Fred's vulnerability. She viewed it as a sign of weakness—just as she saw her own vulnerability as weakness. In her mind, a "strong" man should always feel self-assured and be the one to confidently take charge.

Fortunately, her friends urged her to stay with the relationship, and as it deepened, Jenny came to see Fred's vulnerability not as a weakness, but as a natural by-product of his sensitivity. Fred's willingness to express his feelings allowed Jenny to trust and respect him in a way she had never experienced with a man. As Jenny describes it, "It took a little getting used to, but I really do like how open Fred is with me. I know I don't lose any of my strength when I tell him he hurt my feelings or that I need some reassurance, and I've come to enjoy his being able to do the same. In a funny way, when I compare him to a lot of other men, he actually seems stronger. Other men have the same feelings, but they just don't have the courage to talk about them."

A relationship is a delicate balance of initiative, decision-making, and sensitivity toward one's partner's needs. In recent years, women have moved toward a fuller and more active participation in all aspects of relationships. And men, at least some of them, have made their adjustments to these positive changes. The difficulty is that sometimes sensitivity and decisiveness crash head-on. Women may expect to participate fully, but they also are frequently more respectful of the "take-charge" sort of man.

Adam, a 34-year-old manager of a utilities company, observed, "It isn't always easy for me to plan things for a date. I like to do something that will be interesting and I like to make the decision jointly. But so often she defers to me. 'Where would you like to have dinner?' What I've gotten into doing recently is just arbitrarily picking some restaurant and saying, 'If it's convenient, I'll pick you up at eight—I've made reservations at the Palm.' I get the feeling that women are more comfortable when I handle it that way."

This essentially uncontrolling man has learned to avoid being seen as weak or wishy-washy by women. But something is lost here for the women—his natural inclination to invite participation and the richer experience it would provide to their relationship.

Nice Is Not Romantic

He's sweet and dependable. I know I could count on him for just about anything. He's so nice, but ... there's no excitement." A woman may experience a man as being kind, responsible, and caring—not a bad combination—but she may ultimately lose interest if there is no dynamic tension, no excitement or mystery.

Romance makes us feel transformed, excited, alive, attractive, vibrant. Even the terms used to describe the feeling of falling in love are revealing: chemistry, electricity, sparks flying. Feelings like these give us a sense of aliveness that is totally different from our usual state of mind. If we merely feel someone is nice, we don't experience these ecstatic states.

"He was great, super-nice, and said he thought I was wonderful. He's the kind of guy maybe I could see myself married to someday when I want to settle down—but he sure isn't the type I want to date."

We expect to feel intense and wonderful emotions when we begin a relationship. If those feelings are not there, we don't even feel neutral. In the absence of romance, we actually feel a letdown, an emptiness, a sense of disappointment. There is a simple reason for this. Our mate is, among other things, a reflection of our worth, a measure of our value, our attractiveness. If a man appears dull or predictable, a woman may fear that she too will appear dull, uninteresting, or, God forbid, boring.

The idealized romantic male stereotype is supposed to be fascinating, dynamic, and a bit mysterious. To the extent a man doesn't possess those qualities, a woman may perceive him as "less than," which can result in the woman also feeling "less than." Even though the man may have many other good qualities, if he is not seen as "romantically interesting," the woman frequently depreciates him and so too the value of any relationship she has with him.

Too often we don't value that which we have. We tend to value or idealize that which we long for.

Love and Longing

Joanne, 39, is a hair stylist and makeup artist at an exclusive women's salon. In her early twenties, she had roles in a number of films, and she still acts in an occasional commercial or stage play. Joanne has obsessions, not relationships. Unrequited love is her passion. Last year, her obsession was the TV reporter husband of one of her customers. She had a brief affair with Warren, which he ended, saying she was "far too intense" for him. Undaunted, Joanne pursued him with notes, phone calls, and extravagant presents. She finally forced a confrontation between Warren, his wife, and herself. The wife's hurt and anger at both Warren and Joanne got through to her. Joanne realized that her obsessions were hurting not only herself, but others as well. Suddenly, her "passions"seemed like idiocy, and she sought help.

Joanne has come to understand that unrequited love is a device she uses to avoid forming a close relationship with a caring man. Over the past few months, she has been seeing one man regularly. She has resisted the impulse to run away from him a number of times and seems to be getting beyond the familiar breaking point at which she would run to the next new affair.

Love and longing may seem the same, but they're not. One is nourishment; the other is a hunger. To love someone in a healthy way is replenishing, partly because the act of giving love, in itself, makes us feel good. We like ourselves when we're giving and unselfish. It is, of course, doubly rewarding when our love is accepted and acknowledged—most rewarding of all when it is reciprocated.

Longing is something else. Longing is a hunger for that which we would like but do not have. It is a plea to be loved in return, or at least to be recognized. It is the tension created by the elusiveness or unavailability of the person for whom we long.

Love and longing are confused and mistakenly linked. Longing or unrequited love is an extremely powerful feeling. As noted earlier, such longings are frequently experienced at an early age. Girls not blessed with affectionate fathers may develop intense feelings of longing for the father's contact and love. As these girls become more verbal and can label their experiences and feelings, they come to believe that "longings" and "love" are one. In essence, an identity is established between "wanting" and the concept of love. Obviously, this unfortunate confusion can lead to problems in adult relationships. Women who confuse longing with love find it difficult to feel "in love" if their feelings toward a man are reciprocated. They associate love not with "having" but with "wanting." As one woman explains her feelings, "I was crazy about him as long as I was uncertain about his feelings toward me. But as soon as he committed himself to me, I lost interest." Frequently, expressions of returned love from a man, rather than being accepted with joy, are experienced as disappointing. They diminish the feeling of longing which is associated with love.

In therapy, women of this description can be extremely articulate in defining love and describing what they are looking for in a relationship. But they unfortunately remain unaware that the real hook for them is "wanting" rather than "having." Unless they recognize and change this pattern, they continue to play out this no-win game.

Solutions adopted by such women usually take one of two forms. Some women move from man to man, rejecting each one as soon as he is sure of his love. Such a woman will always find a "good" reason to get out as the man moves closer and demonstrates he is becoming more committed. Other women may resolve such internal conflicts by continually seeking out men who are unavailable. Because their love for such men is not reciprocated, these women can remain in that exquisitely miserable state of longing.

Nice men are not elusive, unknown, or mysterious. They're right there. They are predictable. They call when they say they will. And yet these men are often passed over because they don't stimulate that sense of longing so often linked with the feeling of being in love. Unfortunately, many men and women seem addicted to the state of longing and are unable to embrace genuine love.

Why Some Men Seem Exciting

Let's state one thing at the outset: Some men are more exciting, dynamic, and interesting than others. What are the qualities that lead to these descriptions? Physical appearance is usually not a determining factor. Of course, we all have physical preferences and standards of attractiveness, but for most women, they're not automatically linked to the notion of excitement or fascination. Often the converse seems true. The intriguing man may be characterized as offbeat, masculine, rugged, mysterious. So we know that looks are not germane to this particular issue.

What do women find exciting, then? Someone who is bright, successful, and daring, someone who possesses style, charisma, and mystery. Often a man is seen as interesting by virtue of his celebrity, fame, or power. Stripped of his fame, Woody Allen would certainly not be regarded as a knockout by most women. But there are men who do possess these characteristics. Certainly most women would regard Paul Newman as an exciting or fascinating man, even if he were stripped of his movie credits.

But the critical ingredient for excitement is not good looks, but mystery, coupled with one or more positive traits. The combination of mystery with a compelling positive trait creates a sense of intrigue and curiosity. The tension between these two forces becomes a magnet for men and women—and particularly for women, who tend to be more daring than men with the opposite sex.

Because we are all products of our training and background, some important differences between men and women bear on this point. As noted earlier, women in general seek out states of tension, challenge, and excitement in relationships because as girls they were geared to see relationships as a primary goal in life. Boys, on the other hand, were taught to look for excitement in their jobs and in athletic competitions and so tend to view relationships as less primary. Most men don't look to relationships for excitement and thrills. In fact, they tend to be much more cautious and apprehensive about intrigue and mystery in the opposite sex. Women are more prone to rush into dangerous emotional situations while men tend to avoid possible rejection and danger.

Some qualities in men that women find interesting don't have very interesting underpinnings. Men are self-protective in their contact with women and have a need to disguise their fears and anxiety. They may mask their self-protectiveness in attractive, even stylish, ways. Because of their early programming, men need to appear unruffled and blasé, even though they may feel excited, uncertain, or insecure about a woman.

Another component of this disguise is aloofness and a need to appear unpredictable. Again, all of these traits are directly related to discomfort and anxiety on the part of the man but are often interpreted by the woman as intriguing. So what is, in fact, a limitation in the man can be seen by women as an asset. Why are women so easily deceived?

Gaps in specific information about men create vacuums into which women's fantasies flow. The masked or mysterious man naturally makes sure to leave plenty of gaps, because he isn't quite sure just what a woman would do, think, or feel if he revealed himself to her honestly. Many women know what this game is all about. Even though they may complain that they want to get close, to know him better, they in fact subtly communicate that aloofness is intriguing.

There is no doubt that exciting men are interesting. The problem is that the qualities that translate as exciting in a man are formed more from his fears than from positive, nurturing attributes that hold up over time. Many women relate excitement more to withheld than to openly communicated information. The exciting man actually promises less than meets the eye.

Bad Boys Can Be Fun . . . at Least for a While

Why is it that girls are often drawn to "rascals" or the bad guys in school? The most engaging adolescent characters are often like Marlon Brando or James Dean—outsiders, loners, the angry ones. They're typically seen as not really bad, but independent, rebellious, misunderstood. In high school these boys were the more dominant and popular kids. They had the mystique, and they knew it. While not popular in the conventional sense, they were held in awe by others, including the conventionally popular boys. They were the ones mothers told their daughters to avoid. They did "bad" things. They were daring nonconformists. To "nice" girls who were told to behave in especially proper ways, these boys took on added excitement and mystery. Girls felt these boys knew about risk-taking. They were in touch with the darker side of life. Being with them made girls feel, even if only vicariously, freer and more alive. The movie *Bonnie and Clyde* reflects this urge, the woman's desire to rebel, to hook up with the bad guy and act out her forbidden wishes. In fact, there are thrills to be had with this kind of boy. Even his adult version can be fun, but typically the excitement is short-lived.

Much of the bad boy's appeal is superficial. Although they could take chances, these were boys who had difficulty expressing tender feelings or acknowledging fears. But they were very apt at disguising fears with a protective mask, as is typical of adolescent boys.

Most bad boys eventually grow up, but some of them become "rats."

Who Is the Rat?

Let's face it. All too often, we find the rat to be a charming character. Throughout history, the "rake" or the "rogue" has been romanticized, and even today both men and women ascribe special powers and talents to him.

Furthermore, there still is a double standard that exists because of our sexist upbringing. Women who have a "bad reputation" are not seen as desirable, whereas a man with a "bad reputation" is often an object of intrigue and fascination. Many women are thus drawn to this type of man, despite the inherent dangers, because the rat is such a conquest, a real badge of victory for the woman.

The foremost talent possessed by the rat is his highly developed understanding of women. He has studied the nature of his subject so thoroughly that he knows them well—at least those aspects that are relevant to him. He's no clod. In fact, he may be more intuitive and sensitive than most other men. Unfortunately, though, his basic needs mean more to him than any sense of ethics toward women.

When he was a young boy, he may have had a seductive but emotionally distant mother. This mother stimulated a yearning in him for closeness to her, coupled with fear of her because she never really provided the love he needed. Because he had to study her to know how and when to get the comfort and affection he needed, he developed a heightened perceptiveness and sensitivity to women. Unfortunately, rats know more about women than most nice guys do.

The rat knows how to please a woman, to make her feel special and beautiful. For example, when he is talking to a woman in a restaurant or at a party, he gives all of his attention to her. He can make her feel fascinating. He knows how to stimulate and flatter. He'll make her feel that she has a quick, intelligent sense of humor, that her thoughts are delightful, original, and engaging. Like most good salesmen, he is a wonderful listener. Remember, he must succeed. This is a high-stakes game he's playing and he is going to win—regardless.

Bob, a 34-year-old photographer, fits the mold. "I know just what they want to hear. I know that every woman wants to feel special and that she's dying to feel sexy, and that there's some part of her that's beautiful. I can make her feel like she's the most desirable woman I've ever met. I don't really feel I'm conning anyone, because I believe what I'm saying. I actually do feel that I'm falling in love. At that moment, I really do feel warmth and caring."

The truth is that Bob is falling not for a woman, but for the ecstasy of the moment. The woman and her reactions are merely a mirror for himself. The more she responds, the more his worth and attractiveness are validated. Once he has drained a woman, used up the novelty of her response to him, he must move on. During lovemaking he may say, "I love you," and mean it for that moment. But he doesn't care about the long-term consequences of his actions on his partner. She is slowly but surely being taken in by his ritualistic conquest. And she thinks she is winning, that she has captured her prize.

What kind of woman falls for this? She is a woman who has allowed her emotional hunger to cloud her perceptions. And he knows it! He plays into her secret wish for the perfect man. He becomes that man, and then he promises, dangles, and suggests that he will love her. Here is the magic combination: the perfect man promising his perfect, romantic, intense love. But her need to believe creates a fatal flaw. She ignores the fact that he never delivers.

It's a bit of a paradox that the woman who is highly selective and cautious is often the one who gets involved with the rat. Because of her long-standing wariness, she has pent-up needs for closeness and affection. The powerful chemistry with this type of man can be overwhelming. She is extremely vulnerable to his seduction. He knows she's cautious and plays to this quality. For example, this is not a man who selfishly and clumsily tries to end the evening in bed. He's patient, and can wait. On the surface, he's charming, engaging, and sensitive—just the man to stimulate that condition we call "chemistry." He doesn't really want to hurt anyone. But he does, because he never delivers the long-term goods. He usually fades out, and that's when the pain begins. But while the relationship is going on, it's delightful and fresh.

Even his tendency to fade out acts as an enticement. He knows women are wary of needy men, that they don't want to be with a mama's boy. Therefore, he's clever enough to fade in and out with a rhythm designed to make himself appear strong and self-sufficient and to ensure the maximum enticing tension.

Bob is very aware of this. "After a wonderful evening, I'll send flowers or leave a message, but I won't get together again for at least a week." Why? "That kind of pacing makes me appear as though I have matters to attend to or maybe another woman in my life. I'm self-assured enough to wait for our next encounter—I'm not desperate."

The Magnetism of the Rat

How do women get involved with the rat? Some women thrive on a dangerous combination of needs: longing, mystery, and adventure. These compelling emotional forces lead women to involvement in unhealthy and unfulfilling relationships with men who are ungiving but not uninteresting. There are three basic types of rats that some women find irresistible: the Don Juan, the Elusive Lover, and the Married Rat.

THE DON JUAN ■ Melinda, a 30-year-old art gallery curator, has yet to recover from her three-week romance with an artist as famous for his reputation as a ladies' man as for his sculptures—nudes, of course. "I knew his reputation and should have realized it was just a fling," she says. Yet Melinda, a very sophisticated woman, succumbed to this man's wit and charm and was devastated when he stopped calling. "I wanted to be the one he would stay with, the one who was different. It was great, being with him. I really miss him."

Julie, 35, is a fabric designer who owns an expensive home in a Southern California beach town. For the past two years, she has had an on-again, off-again relationship with Grant. He's a handsome investor, 42, who inherited a substantial amount of money and has held on to very little of it. He has been married four times, each time more briefly. He barreled through the most recent marriage and divorce —to a 22-year-old model—since Julie has known him. In addition to his wives, he has had many affairs and typically is seeing three or four women at a time.

Julie finds him stimulating, complex, and sweetly vulnerable, but frightened of any real commitment—attributes similar to those possessed by her father. Julie has been in therapy long enough to recognize this connection, yet she cannot bring herself to stop seeing Grant. His elusiveness and the high drama of his very tangled love life keep her hooked to him and bored by men who are honestly available.

The Don Juan craves the company and approval of women. Their recognition boosts his self-esteem. Unlike the average ladies' man, he is driven to get his "fix" as often as possible. Since, as in all addictions, the thrill of the capture wears off quickly, he is invariably disappointed and bored and must go off in search of his next conquest.

So what is the magic these men possess, the pull that attracts so many women? First, the Don Juan is seen as "the prize." His image is dazzlingly attractive. He is the personification of power, charm, and tenderness—a "real catch." All women have fantasies about the ideal mate, and with his bag of tricks, the Don Juan builds an image as convincing, compelling, and illusory as a shimmering desert mirage. He appears to be everything a woman wants and needs him to be.

Still another facet of this man's fascination is his ability to make a woman feel valued and cherished. He brings a sense of uniqueness and magic to the relationship and often validates what the woman has always wanted to believe about herself, what she had hoped such a man would recognize someday. She needs to trust what he is saying, doing, and promising. She needs to believe he is for real.

The Don Juan's attraction in a more general way stems from women's misguided wishes to find and believe in the attributes he promises. Such wishes become so strongly attached to these men that women will frequently disregard indications that the Don Juan is not only less than perfect but actually hurtful to them. So, afraid to give up the wish for perfection and face the resulting disillusionment, some women cling to their pursuit, secretly knowing they are leading with their blind side forward.

THE ELUSIVE LOVER ■ The Elusive Lover is less exotic but perhaps more lethal than the

Don Juan. Beth, 31, a charge nurse in a large hospital, has had a sporadic affair with one of the staff doctors for about one year. His ease in dealing with patients and the respect she felt for his commitment to healing first caught her attention. She began seeing him and soon felt that this was the relationship she had always wanted. Beth adjusted her schedule to meet his and would stay up nights waiting for him to drop by to make love. She discovered quite by accident that he was seeing several other women. When she angrily confronted him, he replied, "That's just who I am. If you can't handle it, then don't see me." She decided to handle it—or rather, to put up with it.

Beth probably wouldn't admit it, but she secretly feels her lover really does care for her and that if she waits long enough and tries hard enough he will come around. And he certainly does his share of encouraging those wishes, by maintaining just the right balance between being tantalizingly close and yet disturbingly incapable of capture.

This rat is not nearly as slick as the Don Juan but in many ways he is more insidious and has more staying power. The Don Juan is like a brilliant and colorful flare, quick to ignite and give promise with its light and just as quickly gone. The Elusive Lover, by contrast, has the ability to create and somehow maintain a level of promise and hope. But he never really comes through.

Ginger, who at 29 manages a sporting goods store, met Craig, a research biologist, two years ago when they both competed in a triathlon. She was drawn to him immediately. He impressed her as being strong, unconventional, complex. Craig told her he had been "wounded deeply" in a previous relationship, a fact which she now uses to explain to herself his difficulties with commitment and intimacy.

He is never where he is supposed to be at any given time and occasionally disappears for days at a time—he won't call and he doesn't answer the phone at his house. Ginger excuses his insensitivities about time and place as "artistic temperament." She loves the way they are sexually, and feels his hunger shows that he will eventually give her more than his body.

Although never faithful himself, Craig rants and raves at the mere suggestion that Ginger might be seeing someone else. Petulant and stormy, he demands his freedom but always holds out a vague promise for their future.

Ginger believes that if anyone can make him happy, she can. With the kind of love and understanding only she can provide, she will win him over at last, regardless of what it takes or how long.

Even with his obvious flaws and selfishness,

Craig possesses a kind of charm that creates the illusion he will somehow change—given enough time, understanding, and love. Although he would never say it directly, he makes Ginger feel, with his words and actions, that all he needs is the right person in his life. She, of course, believes she is that right person and will doggedly hang on until she proves it.

A woman's quest for drama and excitement frequently sends her in pursuit of men who are unavailable, even though she refuses to believe it. The Elusive Lover provides a wonderful partner for this woman. The only thing he can truly be relied on for is to remain undependable and unavailable.

Janet, an executive secretary, has had an exquisitely tortured relationship with Barry, a film executive, for three years. Their relationship is what you might call an after-hours thing. Barry typically "drops by" after he is through working (dining, drinking, hustling clients at the latest movie-industry watering hole). They have never been out on a real date! He tells her that going out is too similar to his work and that what he enjoys is just relaxing with her at home.

Janet and Barry have a tumultuous relationship. She complains about how little he gives. "If I'm really honest with myself I know all he wants is to come over and get laid with no demands and then go home." On six different occasions, Janet has told Barry not to call or come by anymore. She has even changed her phone number as many times. Equally often, however, she calls him and starts the whole process over. Janet is fully aware she will continue to feel rejected and lousy about herself. Why?

Janet believes she can ultimately capture Barry and that he is capable of actually engaging in a relationship. She has so dedicated herself to this pursuit that she cannot allow the truth to even approach awareness. The truth is that Barry may be a very competent film executive, and certainly is alluring at a distance, but he is totally incapable of and uninterested in having a relationship with her.

THE MARRIED RAT ▪ The Married Rat is another variety of the same species. Similar to the men described above, he also possesses the critical element for intrigue—he is off limits, taken. Paula, a 34-year-old systems analyst, has been having an affair with Ralph, her boss, for over a year.

"I feel so bad for him. He stays in this bad marriage out of guilt and responsibility for his kids. His wife doesn't understand the kind of pressures he feels. And he says they haven't had a sex life for years. I know I'd make him so much happier, and I don't understand why he won't leave her. Of course, I'm not pushing it—not yet, anyway."

Paula will hang in there with Ralph for a long time, convinced that she is the "right woman" and willing to do just about anything to prove it.

The "right woman" notion is quite common and is certainly encouraged by the typical Married Rat. He is always somehow misunderstood by the woman at home and luxuriates in the sympathy, understanding, and attention he gets from his "other woman." He is convincing when he promises to leave his wife. He may even believe what he's saying, for part of him would like to be free of the responsibilities of marriage. He would love to be single again and off on a new adventure. However, the single most important characteristic of the Married Rat is that while he frequently promises to, he seldom leaves home.

Again, the compelling adhesive in this type of relationship is the "other woman's" difficulty in either understanding or relinquishing her wish for the perfect man. She ignores this man's obvious flaws and deceits. She explains them away, or worse, pins them on his wife. Her need not to be disappointed, not to find out that this man has no intention to follow through, sets up real disappointment. Her foolish blind spot prolongs her losing crusade.

The Pursuit of the Rat

Some women still want to capture one of these elusive men. Such women may not be neurotic, but simply gamblers, risk-takers. We all have within us the desire to tempt the fates. One need only consider the popularity of soap operas, the explosion of romance novels, and the eye-catching articles in magazines such as *Cosmopolitan* to see that there is a huge market in the thrills and dangers of forbidden love.

There are many women who choose to court the dangers we've been describing. Andrea is one. She sincerely believes the chase is worth the possible pains and disappointments. "I like being on the prowl for men who promise real intensity and high drama. Why not? I know how to play the same games, maybe even better."

She knows how to flirt, charm, and entice. Rather than play the helpless coquette, she's the femme fatale. She knows how to let out enough line to make sure the hook is set properly. "You have to keep them wanting more, not running from you. I never leave a party with a man I've just met. And rather than giving a man my phone number, I'll take his. I like to keep the ball in my court."

If a woman insists upon going after one of these rats, she must know her quarry even better than he knows her. To continue to attract the Don Juan she must understand his need to win. She must never fully succumb to his strategies. Part of her must be on guard at all times. If she can do this, he will keep coming back for more. She must let him do the chasing. But remember, it can be a lousy way to live, because the woman can't ever let on how much she really cares for or needs him.

The phenomenon of pursuit is of primary importance in the continued enticement of the rat. The Don Juan is involved in an endless search. Conquests never truly satisfy him; they only stimulate his desire for a new partner. This rat is perhaps the most difficult to corner because the women he selects hungrily fall for his intensity and ardent charms. And as quickly as they whisper, "Yes, yes . . ." he is gone and on the trail of yet another eager, willing victim.

Even with the more tenacious Elusive Lover, pursuit is the clue. The woman who wants to hold on to such a man must learn how to make him as crazy as he makes her—maybe even crazier. She must set aside her feelings of lov-

ing and wanting. She must learn to successfully disguise her needs, wishes, and dreams.
Never showing need, she must make herself
appear somewhat distant, aloof, and unobtain-
able. This will drive any self-respecting rat
into a frenzied battle plan designed to break
down her defenses and capture her heart.

The difficulty with this strategy is not that
it doesn't work, because it does, but that it is
so tiring over any length of time. Nothing is
quite so exhausting as living a lie, which is
exactly what a relationship with this man must
be. Remember, to hold on to this type of man,
a woman can never let on how much his lack
of commitment hurts her, or how much she
really cares.

Still another problem in dealing with this
rat is that the woman who does so must actively diminish her emotional expression and
assume an elusive posture. She must forget
about having an equal give-and-take relationship. She must always be on her guard not to
let on how strongly she feels. Nor can she
freely express anger or indignation for ways in
which he hurts, betrays, and disappoints her,
because these expressions reveal caring in the
sting of her tears.

The Married Rat is somewhat different from
the others in that he does commit himself—
that is, until the demands and ultimatums be-

gin. To captivate this rat, the woman cannot make demands that call for a decision on his part. As long as she refrains from insisting, "Your wife or me!" the relationship will continue.

One thing is clear—this rat is not leaving his wife, for whatever reason. To retain his interest, his lover must not make him feel too torn or too guilty. This rat's lover must appear to be content. She must understand that she comes second to his family. Christmas, Thanksgiving, New Year's Eve, will be spent with his family. Even birthdays are no guarantee—his wife may have other plans for him on that night.

The Married Rat feels miserable at home and always tells his lover about it. It is extremely important for her to take heed of his misery. The lover must concede where the wife demands, tolerate where the wife gets angry, love and understand in circumstances where the wife insists on reform. This contrast will underscore the misery and resentment he feels toward his wife and run up points on the side of the lover.

If the Married Rat does leave his wife, there is a strong possibility that what he did to her he may also do to his lover. The lover may have been the "excuse" to leave the marriage, but his need for freedom may include eventual freedom from his lover as well.

Are they really worth a woman's time and love? These men are interesting, and they do stimulate intense feelings of aliveness and vibrancy in women. They really have so many genuinely fascinating characteristics that it is too bad they fade so soon. Or maybe that is not so bad—maybe the fade is part of the charm, challenge, and excitement. Such a man can be fun, mysterious, and make sincere promises, but, beneath all the golden shimmer is still a rat.

CHAPTER SIX

Men Who Make Women Want to Scream

There are several types of men who very predictably end up infuriating women. Some are charming in the beginning and then change. Others are attractive because of the qualities women hope to find in them. All, sooner or later, make women want to scream in frustration.

The Clam

Some men radiate a tough mystique that grows out of a basically selfish, withholding, and guarded nature. This kind of man can be as dangerous as he is attractive and intriguing. A woman can be drawn to what she sees as strength in this man's insensitive toughness and may also feel potentially reassured by that "strength." We say "potentially," because she never quite feels part of such a man's strength, since the man doesn't really share or even truly open himself to the woman. He makes the woman do the emotional work for the two of them. He sets the stage and she dances around, attempting to read his mind. She knows she wants the security of feeling close to his strength. But he doesn't ever allow her to get too close. She loves it, she hates it. She knows she is drawn by the very characteristic she is bound and determined to change.

Arlene, 28, is a warm, gregarious bank loan officer. When she met Tom she knew this relationship was "it" for her. She described him as "a bit too emotionally guarded" for her tastes, but she thought all that would change once he realized he could trust her. She thought that she understood Tom's secretive tendencies, which she saw as reflecting his self-control or perhaps shielding an old hurt. He wasn't the least sensitive to her needs, but she talked herself into believing it was only because she hadn't communicated them to him clearly enough, and so it must be her fault.

They married eight months after they met. Arlene felt sure the kind of commitment they were making would open the door to at last feeling loved by Tom. She was absolutely convinced that if she loved him enough, with no holds barred, he would open himself to her. With love as the key, she would open his heart and finally reap the treasure that surely lay within. It was certainly a nice fantasy—but it never happened. Tom's tough, controlled outer shell concealed a tough, controlled inner core. Tom claimed he loved Arlene, but she never felt it and he never showed the demonstrative affection she wanted and needed. She divorced him after one painful year.

Arlene made a mistake in the choice of her relationship with Tom. She interpreted his guarded, withholding nature as mystique. What she found was that instead of standing guard over some hidden treasure, he in fact was desperately trying to protect his insecurity from exposure. When Arlene realized this, Tom's strength was transformed in her eyes to brittle crumbling defenses. His wonderful mystique turned to fear.

The Clam either fears his dependency needs or has managed to convince himself that he doesn't have any. He is very attractive to many women, who mistake this trait for strength and self-containment. But problems soon emerge as the woman begins to want more. We all experience love, at least in part, through feeling needed by our partner, "needed" emotionally. The Clam can't allow himself to need anyone enough to form an intimate, satisfying bond. To do so would require confronting his fears of weakness and vulnerability. Ancient, scarred-over hurts may have destroyed his capacity to feel that deeply.

We all need, in a love relationship, to have our partners dependent upon us—not blood-suckingly so, but needing us emotionally nevertheless. And this man will never allow himself to be dependent enough to be able to form a close, sharing relationship. He functions as a self-contained system. No matter how warm a woman's love, it will never melt his protective shield. It is too tough, too old.

Another necessary bonding agent in the man/woman relationship is trust. Trusting and being trusted. The Clam is recognized by his secretive qualities. The secretive person is protecting something he fears may be lost, betrayed, taken away. Women need to keep in mind when they meet a secretive man that his concealment is a result of his past and has nothing to do with them.

Trust develops through a process of give and take. It involves mutually disclosing deeper and more complex aspects of ourselves. The Clam cannot take a chance on important emotional exposure. He will not risk the danger of looking into old wounds stored away in the locked file of forgotten, painful memories. Most often, he doesn't even know just what it is he is protecting or even that he is, in fact, behaving in a self-protective and distrustful fashion. The Clam cannot trust and he does not open up.

He doesn't know how to love, for the process of giving and loving means exposing his needs and vulnerabilities. If he hasn't learned to love by the time he is an adult, a woman won't be able to teach him—no matter how patient she is. It's foolish to believe otherwise.

What is misguided in the pursuit of this man is the failure to correctly identify his real strengths and weaknesses. If you find yourself with this type, you may believe you possess the magic potion to change him, to release in him what you believe to be a capacity to love, but you don't. In fact, the more a woman loves and cares for this kind of man, the better the chances of driving him away. Intimacy is his enemy—it scares the hell out of him. If he doesn't run away first, you will become so frustrated with having to do all the emotional work, provide all the tenderness, that eventually you will end the relationship—if you're smart.

The Pseudo-Liberated Male

At the outset of a relationship, the Pseudo-Liberated Male can be disarmingly attractive to women. He is the living embodiment of the liberated man, the perfect and natural complement to today's woman. He accepts her changes, even encourages them. He seems gentle and sensitive, vulnerable, expressive, revealing—a real dream come true! But it's a dream that frequently turns into a nightmare.

This type of man interpreted the women's movement as an invitation to become more expressive emotionally. He distorts this new "freedom" as a license to whine and a rationalization to express endless fears and personal insecurities, often to the point of utter distraction. The Pseudo-Liberated Male is certainly quite different from the withholding man described earlier. Many women see him as a welcome change—someone who will share himself, be open with his feelings. That's great, but some of these men go overboard. Even when women begin to get a whiff of his excesses, they frequently don't trust their own instincts—they don't run.

In a way, women have been encouraged and made to feel as if they should like this man. After all, if they expect to be able to explore new and unfamiliar "masculine" parts of themselves, and if they expect men to accept and love them for it, then they, in turn, should be tolerant of men's becoming more expressive and vulnerable.

When Marv and Marlena came in for couples therapy, Marv said they were not having any specific problems living together—they wanted rather to make their relationship as dynamic and positive as possible, and they were both interested in the therapy process as a means of personal growth.

Marv, 32, is a free-lance carpenter and unpublished novelist. Marlena, 34, is an office administrator for an import-export company and the steady wage earner in their household. They're both active in antinuclear and liberal political causes, Marv more so than Marlena because he doesn't work steadily and has more time.

Marv and Marlena are both bright, attractive, and personable. But what became clear in the very first session, as Marv talked on and on, with occasional glances at Marlena for approval, was that Marv is a narcissistic Pseudo-Liberated Male. He wasn't interested in making his relationship with Marlena better. What he wanted was a fresh, larger audience for his seemingly inexhaustible insights about himself.

Marlena revealed that Marv preferred talking about their relationship and himself to just about any other activity. Marlena eventually confessed that she felt exhausted by the constant talk and by his incessant demands for attention and analysis of "where we're at with each other now."

This man hides the fact that he is an emotional drain, that he's a taker. He is so happy and relieved to have a chance to legitimize his insecurity and neediness that he doesn't realize that he is taking without giving. He sincerely believes that his emotional diarrhea is a gift. He hides his fears and passivity beneath a deceptive costume of gentleness and sensitivity —and hopes the woman won't see through his disguises.

During the early stages of the relationship, this man performs dazzlingly. He is a master with words—he may even be poetic. His verbal output is such that a woman thinks she should feel nourished. Instead, she feels drained. He wraps his need for reassurance in a pretty package, one that can make a woman feel privileged, needed. Eventually, she may become aware that all he ever seems interested in talking about is the relationship—or himself! She wants to like him. She thinks she should like him. After all, he is expressive, isn't he? "In touch" with his feelings? Why does he make her want to scream? Perhaps it's because she finally realizes that he would rather talk about a relationship than have one.

These men are sensitive, and that can be a refreshing experience. The problem is that as time goes by, it becomes increasingly apparent that their sensitivity is one-sided, directed consistently toward themselves.

We believe women do want to know how a man feels, but they don't want to hear about it all the time. A relationship with one of these overly emotional types can eventually make them feel crazy. Somewhere along the way, these women may sense they are drawing a curtain of insensitivity about themselves, much as they have accused men of doing in the past. They want to shout, "Will you just shut up and make love to me and stop this endless discussion about us?" "Where we're at" with this man is all too frequently talking about his feelings toward you, toward himself, and toward the relationship—"talking about" rather than letting it just happen.

The Clam is too contained, while the overly sensitive Pseudo-Liberated Male is too uncontained. He wears his insecurities like medals on his chest.

Trying to free this man from his emotional problem can make a woman feel powerful, but it's a trap. They are better left alone. You might even be doing them a favor, for then they would be forced to deal with their insecurities themselves, from the inside out, rather than attempting to foist the responsibility on some woman who will indulge them.

Some men who make women want to scream are fundamentally unredeemable. The smart woman passes on these men, regardless of how interesting or intriguing they may appear on the surface. The Clam and the Pseudo-Liberated Male are such men. Then there are two other types of men who are terribly frustrating to women, but who do have very redeemable features if a woman can tolerate the frustration and make her way through the obstacles they place in her way: the Perpetual Adolescent and the Walking Wounded.

The Perpetual Adolescent

The Perpetual Adolescent stopped developing in what is late adolescence for a man—around the mid-twenties. This man's unspoken and unconscious credo is "I'm going to be 25 forever." This stunted growth is not always easy to detect. It is reflected in his emotional construction and in his diminished capacity to participate fully in relationships rather than in the external surface features of his life.

Outwardly, he has many disarmingly attractive qualities. He may be boyish in a confident, brash way. This man often works with the public and is articulate, with an easy, charming manner. He makes people feel comfortable.

Greg, a handsome, athletic yacht broker, lives in an expensive condominium overlooking a marina. From his sundeck, he can see his sailboat bobbing in its slip as well as the pool and tennis courts crowded with tanned single men and women. At 36, Greg still considers himself young and needing to devote most of his time and energy to building his career. He feels no pressure to marry. In fact, he tells himself, as well as more than an occasional woman, that he needs more time before settling down—time for his work, time for travel, time to "have fun."

Greg describes his life-style as "fun." He jogs and works out daily. He looks youthful, tanned and toned. He dresses fashionably. He tells himself there's no hurry, plenty of time to find his "ideal woman."

Actually, these are excuses for Greg to live in a perpetual adolescence. He talks about responsibility and commitment but runs when a woman starts to demand it. He can be affectionate to a woman and mean it, but he is not willing to grow up and relate to her as an adult. When his relationships get to the stage where it is natural for them to move to a deeper level, Greg becomes frightened and pulls away. He typically dismisses the woman as "dependent, clingy, possessive, demanding," rather than facing his own fear and reluctance to enter adulthood. He is blind to his profound reluctance to mature, for his youthful posture serves as a shield and defense against intimacy.

The Perpetual Adolescent's greatest fear is entrapment, for he doesn't fully trust his own autonomy. "To have to give" and "to be able to receive" both detonate deep, underlying fears of dependency in him. This man hides his fears of intimacy from himself by coming very close to committing in a relationship. But he ultimately wards off those fears by always making sure that "very close" is only that, not marriage.

The Perpetual Adolescent has rather shallow views and interactions with women. For that matter, his friendships with men are equally shallow. He often perceives himself as an adventurer. But the greatest adventure of all—marriage—is an event he is never quite yet ready for.

Initially, he can be captivating, for he has fine-tuned many aspects of his external presence. He can trot out all the phrases that make him sound wonderful and make a woman feel wonderful. The trouble is, he's a deal opener, not a deal closer. The Perpetual Adolescent is extremely frustrating to women, for as they naturally want to deepen what seems like a nicely developing relationship, he slowly pulls away. If he only did something truly rotten, she could free herself and be glad to be rid of him. But he doesn't—maddeningly, his only real flaw is his unwillingness to grow up.

We have said that this man is redeemable, and he is. Given enough time and patience, most men eventually do grow up, marry, and have families. For this type of man, the critical age seems to be about 39. He begins to panic when he is unable to deny being middle-aged. Having learned to trust his own independence more solidly, he is less afraid of entrapment and connection. He has become acutely aware of his own mortality, and he doesn't want to become a lonely old man.

While we wouldn't recommend the younger version of this man, the older model isn't bad at all. Should you know someone like this and want to deepen the relationship, there are a couple of important factors to keep in mind.

This man, even though he fears it, is capable of becoming healthily dependent on a woman. The mistake most women make is in not understanding that he does need a woman and can make a connection. Typically, the woman pushes too quickly and succeeds only in pushing him away. It is not that the impulse to move forward is inappropriate on the woman's part, for it isn't, but the timing is critical. This man is most likely to connect deeply to the woman who has patience to let him develop a strong need for her first. Then, and only then, should she begin to make her healthy demands for commitment. By then, he is so involved that he wants to stay.

The Walking Wounded

After a separation or divorce, both men and women naturally feel a mixture of hurt, bitterness, and rejection. Fortunately for most of us, these wounds heal over time, and the best medicine is eventually to love again.

Men and women usually suffer equally, but there are wounds unique to men that merit understanding. The Walking Wounded man can drive women crazy for a time, but he does heal and definitely is redeemable. In fact, these men often make fine mates precisely because they are committed to long-term relationships.

There are two basic types of wounds. The most painful is, of course, the loss of one's mate and most likely the loss of family. The other is the loss of financial security resulting from the divorce. The loss of a family structure is devastating to most divorced men. Suddenly, he finds himself alone in an apartment or hotel room, feeling lost, disoriented, and forlorn. He envies his wife, who frequently continues living in the family home, in familiar and, at least in his mind, secure surroundings. For the first time, some men will sadly and poignantly realize how important it was to hear "Daddy" when they came home from work.

Contributing to this sense of isolation that divorced men experience is the constant apprehension that even in his grief, he must continue working hard to make money. There is a line from a western song that goes, "I can't halve my half again." For many men, a divorce means money: the destruction of the financial security and comfortable life-style which they worked so long and hard to create. Women suffer equally from the financial fallout from divorce, but it is our purpose here to acquaint you with the male point of view.

Most men feel "ripped off" after a divorce. Regardless of the validity of this attitude, they are nevertheless embittered by the helplessness they felt during the process of marital dissolution. This helplessness is often in combination with the sense of futility they have regarding child custody. In addition, they have increased financial anxieties related to the demand of separate living expenses. In their anxious and dark moments, they're not sure they can make it.

Even though they may be freer to date than are their wives, they have a sense that it's all a dream. They tend to drink and to abuse drugs, which compounds their depression.

How do these men appear to the women who encounter them? If they are newly separated, they can actually appear quite attractive, because they haven't yet assumed the guarded mantle of men who have been single for a while. They may be vulnerable too, which can be appealing to women, especially those who like to nurture men.

The newly separated man is open, eager to talk and to reveal himself, though too often this evolves into a tedious self-pity which will eventually drive a woman crazy. Even so, his eagerness for contact and relationships is quite appealing to many women.

The recently separated man tends to talk about his ex-wife and bitch about any number of injustices he feels. This facet of him can become so boring that women quickly feel the urge to run. A word of advice: After a while, don't be such a good listener. It's bad for him to wallow in self-pity and definitely not romantic for any woman.

There is a common problem with the Walking Wounded that can break a woman's heart.

A woman may be age 32 to 40 and childless and find herself involved with a divorced man of the same age or older who already has children. It is vitally important for that woman, if she wants children of her own, to make this desire known to the man early in the relationship. Many divorced men are well-meaning but frankly have no desire to start another family. Yet they will mutter vaguely, "Well, if it's really going well, I guess I might want to have another kid." That's not good enough. A woman needs a clear answer or else it's time to move on. To invest precious years in a relationship only to end up with a man who has very different dreams is tragic indeed.

Men who have been separated for a year or more are usually less appealing than the very vulnerable, freshly separated ones we've been exploring. But they often have another kind of attractiveness: They're ripe for the picking. This is true in spite of their seemingly hardened outer shell. Though wary and a bit suspicious about being hurt again, they will become involved. They can make good mates, and do wish genuine intimacy, but they are scared. The solution is simple: Don't push for commitment in the beginning, even the first six months. Women who need reassurances right away will not do well with this type of man. He does need extra time, but not forever. After a period of exclusive involvement, it is appropriate for the relationship to deepen and become more involved. He will commit himself if the woman really means it. But in some cases it may take an ultimatum. The woman who acts as if she will wait forever is making a real mistake, because she will be taken for granted.

One final word on the Walking Wounded. There are women who advise friends and say to themselves, "Stay away from any man who has just come out of a relationship. They just want a nursemaid. As soon as they heal a little, they'll leave you to play the field." It is true that they may be overly dependent at first or need to date around a bit, but some of the best men are not out there very long. Men who have been in a marriage, even a bad marriage, want to be in a relationship again. The best men are not single for long, and shouldn't be dismissed foolishly.

2

GETTING
SMART

CHAPTER SEVEN

Many Special Women, Few Good Men?

———

The second half of this book is about getting smart with men. We want to begin with a brief exploration of a widespread concern that has been characterized as the "great American male shortage." We will propose a new way of interpreting this dilemma, keeping in mind that how you define any problem has important implications for the ways in which you go about solving the problems.

"Where are all the good men?"

"I know lots of single women who are really terrific, but I sure don't know many interesting, desirable single men."

"The unattached men I meet are either workaholics, sports nuts, hung up on their ex-wives,

terminal neurotics, or otherwise single for good
reason."

"I refuse to settle for a man who doesn't
meet my standards, and it sure doesn't seem to
leave many guys to choose from."

We hear these statements every day. We
asked our women clients, our wives, and our
women friends, "Do you think there are more
interesting and desirable single women or
men?" Overwhelmingly, they indicated a sur-
plus of desirable women, a dearth of desirable
men.

Statistically, there *are* more women than men,
and the discrepancy widens with increasing
age. Large urban areas tend to have much heav-
ier concentrations of single women than men.
In fact, conservative estimates suggest that there
are about five single women for every four
available men in many major metropolitan re-
gions. Women who live in large cities are indeed faced with numbers that are stacked
against them. There are significant imbalances,
which helps to explain the despair many women
feel about ever meeting the right man.

The issue, however, doesn't center on sheer
numbers alone, but on the availability of "desirable" men. The problem for women is not
only to find a man, but to find one they perceive as "special." It is our belief that the
difficulty today is not only that there are too

few men, but that there is a shortage at the top. By "top," we mean the relatively small percentage of men who are both materially successful and have attractive personalities, and are therefore universally desirable.

Put another way, it seems that 80 percent of the single women are interested in 20 percent of the available men. That there are more single women than men is undeniable, but what we are seeing is a *real* shortage of men who manage to squeeze through the narrowing filters of today's smart woman's selection process. We believe that given all these factors, smart women need to become more realistic in their expectations if they want to form close long-term relationships with men.

Marrying Up and Marrying Down

Traditionally, women were taught that status might be gained through affiliation with an accomplished man, and this phenomenon plays a major role in the perceived shortage of men. Today, smart women are developing their own potential and achieving power and status in their own right. Nevertheless, many single women, regardless of their level of achievement, continue to feel internal and external pressures to "marry up"—to find someone who is even more powerful, more successful. Men still are seen as a catapult to enhanced status as well as financial security.

Clint recalled, "After I got married, I wanted to fix up my terrific women friends with some of the men I know. After a while, I stopped doing that because I realized none of my male friends were 'good enough' for these women! It came to me that none of them wanted men who were on a career par with them; the men had to be 'better.' For example, I have a friend who is a mid-level executive, and I wanted to introduce him to a woman lawyer friend of mine. They both make about the same money. She declined. When I asked why, she said vaguely that he might be threatened by her career success. I knew he wouldn't be threatened at all, but I realized she had her sights set higher. Her friends insist she deserves a 'real winner.' "

In talking with women and asking them to define their ideal mate, we find that they invariably describe a man they consider superior to them in at least one or two areas. Most women want a man whose earning power is greater than theirs because they still count on the husband to be the major income producer.

This is true even if the woman is an executive with a good job and a substantial income herself.

Many women firmly believe that men "marry down." One old saw goes, "Women marry power, men marry beauty." Sometimes this is said to indicate that men go for looks or are attracted to women whose accomplishments are less, and therefore nonthreatening to the male ego. We believe this is a serious misconception.

When we asked our male clients to describe their ideal mate, they listed a wide range of attributes. A sense of humor, warmth, intelligence, physical attractiveness, trust, honesty, and emotional stability were all ranked high. Certainly women also value and are responsive to the same qualities in men. But for some women they don't seem enough. These attributes must be accompanied by the proofs of material success to qualify a man as mateworthy.

In speaking with men, we didn't find one man who thought he had "married down." Most of these men had attained higher levels of education and did make more money than their wives, but all saw their wives as peers and equals.

Some men, unarguably, are threatened by accomplishment in a woman. But in general they are not. A man who is successful and accomplished in his own right doesn't need his mate's success to enhance his ego or her income to feel secure. What attracts men are qualities that are independent of career success, whereas that same success is enormously important to many women in their selection of a man. This has serious implications for women, especially accomplished women. A woman who has worked hard at an education and career is not necessarily valued higher by men—in particular by the super-successful men she feels she "deserves." Despite this, however, there is an increasing trend among successful men to value the support and real sense of partnership that a self-sufficient and career-oriented woman provides.

Many successful women today are frustrated because the competition for the few men at the top is intense. We're often asked by smart women, "What are men looking for? It seems they just want women who don't threaten them." We don't believe this is true. Men do, however, have a different order of priorities.

Why Married Men Look Better

Many times we hear women comment that the "good ones" are all taken. Or that married men somehow always seem more attractive than single men. There is a simple explanation for this. Married or "attached" men are not that different from single men—they just behave differently. When a man feels secure in a relationship, he is able to act in a much looser, freer fashion with other women; conversely, men and women who are single tend to behave in tighter and more self-conscious ways with each other. This is why the singles-bar scene often seems so shallow and unattractive. Single men and women complain about each other, and yet when the same individuals are met under more relaxed circumstances, they seem much more interesting and desirable. The "good ones" are not all married; it's just that the security and confidence that marriage provides allow them to act in a more natural and relaxed way than their single counterparts. Let those nervous, shy single men find a woman to connect with and they blossom into "good" married men, too.

Self-Fulfilling Prophecies

In the past few years we have seen emerging an unfortunate negative judgment of men by some women. Its general tone is that men are in "bad shape" today. Men are judged less special, less desirable, less interesting than women. While we believe there is some substance to many of these criticisms, we also believe prejudice against males is self-defeating for women, just as male chauvinism diminishes men.

First of all, men do not believe they are as undeveloped, boring, and frozen as some women think. Even if this were true, to approach them with that belief system is to kill the opportunity for anything positive or fresh to happen.

Most men are satisfied with the way they are. Furthermore, they are not complaining about women, for many of them like the changes that have occurred. Today, in fact, as women complain vigorously about the "great American male shortage," men feel rather special, "in demand."

The point here is that criticism and depreciation of men lead nowhere, certainly not with men. Most of us, male or female, are wonderful in some respects and flawed in others. However, many women tend to look for the best in their female friends, and they see the worst in men. There is a kind of double standard operating. Women can overlook flaws in their female friends, but those same imperfections, or even lesser ones, become glaring and intolerable when found in men.

It all depends on your point of view. For every woman who insists that men are too narrow in their interests, there is a man who insists that women have no passion for discussing or analyzing world affairs. Some women may feel men's focus never wavers from their careers, while there are men who cannot fathom women's inability to "really" understand the drama and chesslike quality of a football game. The fact is that if you try to understand the opposite sex, if you look for the best in someone, you will bring out the best. If you expect the worst, you will probably discover it.

Women who let go of negative, self-fulfilling prophecies tend to have more interesting and fulfilling experiences with men. It is refreshing for both men and women when they talk to the opposite sex with the same interest and looseness they do with their friends. Labeling or categorizing people does not allow for the discovery of what might be fresh, delightful, or interesting about them. When we approach someone with a "prove yourself to me" attitude, we're in trouble. Yet, in our experience, single people all too frequently do that with each other. As a result, nothing different or novel happens and there is a lack of richness and variety in social relationships.

It's important to realize that people "on trial" —men or women—don't display their best side. They become tense, dull, and unspontaneous. The way a woman relates to a man can actually change his response to her, so he *becomes* more interesting and desirable.

When cynicism and pessimism are suspended, what may now appear to be a disheartening "male shortage" can look more like an abundance.

CHAPTER EIGHT

Release from
Endless Mourning

Arlene, a 36-year-old set designer for TV variety shows, was miserable after she broke up with Hal, 25, an actor, ten weeks ago. Unable to sleep night after night, she lost fifteen pounds from her already slender frame. This normally attractive, stable, and vivacious woman was literally pining away for Hal, who dropped her without warning for a 22-year-old rock singer.

Thoughts of Hal not only dominated her waking hours but also tormented her dreams— jealousy dreams of confronting Hal with his new girlfriend.

What was certainly as painful as the loss of Hal's love was the humiliation she felt at not being able to rid herself of his memory. She awoke with thoughts and fantasies of what he was doing at that moment. She went to sleep with the same pictures racing through her mind.

The fact that Hal was a regular on a show at the same studio made it even more difficult for Arlene. She found herself compulsively checking his parking space, so she could know whether or not he was on the studio lot. At first, she casually asked mutual friends about him and his new girlfriend as if she no longer cared. More recently, the questions had taken on a nakedly desperate tone. It was very apparent to her friends that Arlene was not letting go. She wrote him letters which she never mailed. She made many late-night phone calls to his apartment, only to hang up when "she" answered.

The final humiliation came one night when she made one of her increasingly frequent drives past his building to see if his lights were on. The windows were dark that evening, so Arlene parked her car on a side street where she could watch the entrance to his building. She fell asleep and was awakened by a tapping on her window. To her horror, it was Hal. Arlene opened her eyes to see his amazed face and "her" not three feet away, sitting in Hal's parked car. Arlene watched, paralyzed, as Hal, shaking his head, turned away. He opened the door for the young woman and pointedly put his arm around her as they walked up the sidewalk.

Glenda, a 30-year-old interior designer, still cried herself to sleep more often than not eight months after her boyfriend Ward fumbled through his final goodbyes. Theirs had been a heady, fast, and volatile relationship. They seemed to share so many interests, particularly their love of the outdoors. They had often gone camping and backpacking and had spent many a glorious sunset together snuggling in front of a campfire in the forest. She introduced Ward to the design world she loved so much. He got her interested in running. Even though Glenda never thought she would ever enjoy running, she quickly developed a strong sense of accomplishment as they silently glided down the beach together during their evening runs.

Glenda felt close and content. But what seemed like near perfection started to crumble when Ward inexplicably began to pull away. Her strong need to understand and to hold him only served to speed his retreat. Before she could even begin dealing with the thought that she was losing Ward, she had lost him.

Glenda couldn't believe that she was alone and that he was really gone for good. She found herself having long dialogues with him in her head—some warm and nostalgic, others hurt and angry, still others raw and pleading. So silent and private was her grief, even her closest friends thought she was handling the situation like a champ. She wasn't.

Restaurants, songs, theaters, even outfits she remembered wearing with him were nagging reminders of his absence. When she was alone, which was almost all the time she wasn't at work, Glenda's thoughts turned to self-recrimination and ceaseless recapitulations of what she might have said or done differently, as if hitting upon that perfect explanation might somehow change things—might magically bring him back.

Glenda explained in session, "I know it's over and that he isn't coming back, but I just keep on thinking about him. I know it's ridiculous to hope, but I do anyway. You want to hear something very embarrassing? There are a lot of nights when I sleep in an old stretched-out jogging suit he left. I put that stupid thing on and pretend he's holding me as I go to sleep."

Jackie, a 28-year-old secretary, broke up with Allen, a journalist, two years ago. Since that time, she has dated many men, but none compare, even come close to, Allen. Jackie believed

he was the one "just right" man for her. Sophisticated and from a family of high achiev-
ers, he seemed to possess all the right qualities.
She loved his family and adopted them as her
own. Jackie also greatly enjoyed Allen's many
and interesting friends, who ranged from struggling artists to political types.

Jackie felt a sense of completion in Allen's
presence. She felt more womanly, sexier, and
more whole than at any other time she could
remember. In her most private and honest moments, however, Jackie had to admit that some
of the sense of perfection in Allen was filled in
by her hopeful, eager wishes. In truth, Allen
was far from perfect.

Allen's one passion was his work. A hot in-
vestigative piece or a month-long war assignment was what made him really come alive.
When it came to relationships, they took a
definite back seat. Jackie talked about her
wishes to get married and have a family; Allen
spoke with excitement about the possibility of
a bureau chief assignment in Beirut. When
Allen was offered and accepted the job over-
seas, Jackie's bright hopes turned to disappointment and despair.

Allen wrote twice a week for the first month
or so, and Jackie answered each letter. Both
were careful to sound casual. Neither wrote of
future plans together. The letters became

shorter, then fewer, then they stopped. Jackie forced herself to see other men, but she felt no one could match Allen or ignite the special feelings she had had when she was with him.

And Jackie was right. Every man she went out with, she compared to Allen. Every one came up short. Jackie soon realized she was looking to find Allen in them, and, of course, he wasn't there. Her dogged search made it impossible for her to see any of the unique qualities her dates did have. Other men didn't fully exist because they were not Allen.

Jackie, sadly, believes Allen is not simply one man she loved, but the "only" man for whom she could have those wonderful, dizzy feelings of love. "I still have fantasies that he will come back and we'll start where we left off. I know that thinking this way is probably not very realistic, but that's the way it is."

These women have one important thing in common: Each is endlessly mourning a lost love. And while the pain these women experience is terribly real and terribly sad, it is also self-defeating. The central difficulty in an extended mourning process is a search not so much for the perfect man, but for the perfect feeling of love.

Although the grieving process must be gone through, we believe the prolongation of this process is related to the difficulty many women have in coming to grips with the issues of victimization and low self-esteem.

The problem of prolonged mourning plagues far more women than it does men. It's certainly not that men are rejected less frequently, or that they feel less pain. The difference lies in their solutions to the problem. Men tend to handle rejection, even from someone they loved deeply, by reconnecting with another woman, often surprisingly quickly. Many women inadvertently attempt to deal with the wound of rejection through continued fantasies about getting back together with the man who rejected them—a self-defeating and painful choice. As we have indicated elsewhere, because connectedness is so central for women, they will take chances and put forth heroic efforts to salvage or restore a relationship.

Believing in Magic

When women fall in love with someone, they tend to impute almost magical qualities to him. The origins of this tendency are to be found in childhood conditionings. As we discussed in the beginning of the book, from early on, women put a heavy emphasis on relationships and attachment. And, being freer with emotional expression, they are more likely to embrace this tendency and thus heighten their emotional response to men. The end result is that they impute almost magical qualities to their lover. By magic we don't mean that the man is seen as flawless; many of these men are quite accurately perceived. The magic comes from the way the woman feels toward the man and the specialness she so generously attributes to him. As Jackie expressed it, "There is something totally unique about him that I know I'll never find in another man. Sometimes I feel like it's silly to go on looking. No one's going to have all those great little quirky things that Allen had, those special qualities that so endeared him to me."

Allen may have been interesting, but he wasn't the man Jackie wanted him to be. He didn't really treat her well when he was around, and he handled the ending of their relationship poorly. Jackie's foolish belief in and search for perfection cause her to discount and ignore Allen's very real shortcomings as a love partner. She is also perpetuating a singular focus on those qualities in him that made her feel good. What makes her loss so endless is her resistance to seeing attractive but different facets in other men and the tenacious fantasy that someday she and Allen will be together again.

Wounded Self-Esteem

It is normal and natural for us to feel bad when we lose someone. Rejection can be a loss more cruel even than death, for it carries with it the painful bite of lost personal esteem and confidence. Although it is quite normal to experience a certain amount of diminished confidence when we are left against our wishes by a loved one, the process of a prolonged mourning of that loss is quite different. The endless component of grief is related directly to a power vested in the man and lost—power to validate a woman's worth as lover, woman, person.

A woman must never give a man the power to determine how she feels about herself. No person should have that sort of power, not under any circumstance, and yet we have seen scores of women left feeling worthless because a man has rejected them.

Women who participate in prolonged mourning typically feel acted upon by life's forces rather than experiencing their own capacity to act. They feel victimized. Men come along and make them feel special, and when they leave, they take away their capacity to feel good about themselves. Instead of seeing deficits in the man, there is a tendency for many women to think *they* were at fault, that *they* did something wrong. This process of self-recrimination serves no useful purpose and only intensifies the agony.

Release to Love Again

The first step a woman must take to get over a lost love is to let go of the magical quality she assigned to the man and the relationship. She must stop thinking that she'll never feel that way again and understand that whatever the relationship was, now there is no relationship, only a phantom afterimage. Only after the notion of "unreal" has been assigned to the relationship is it possible to create the context for new hope.

The second step has to do with assuming more personal responsibility for experience in the world—the whole panoply of feelings, reactions from others, life events. For whatever complex set of reasons, things didn't work out. But it's crucial for a woman to realize that she was not simply a respondent in the relationship, but half of the reason for the chemistry. Without her, the magic would not have existed.

We find that far too many women forget the real importance of cause and effect in the interactive process of a relationship. They lose contact with their own sense of personal power, particularly when they feel powerless to make the man want to stay. They may confuse that temporary sense of power loss with a more long-term and crippling feeling of powerlessness.

A man may leave, but he can't take a woman with him. She and she alone is the owner of her personal worth and essence. No one, not the most clever or most dark-hearted of men, can steal that. It can only be given away.

The recognition, then, of the significance of one's contribution in the relationship is an essential prerequisite for release from prolonged mourning. It clearly signals not simply a wish, but a real and substantial reason to hope for love to happen again.

As we noted earlier, a potent component to prolonged mourning is a tendency to slowly fall prey to allowing the man to validate self-worth. If you find yourself in the grips of this process, you must take back that power of validation and learn to like yourself again. Find new ways to gain positive information and feedback about yourself. Put yourself in positions where you can have access to a variety of direct responses to who you are and how you are perceived. This will probably require new people and certainly new experiences.

Many women affected by rejection find it difficult to seriously address the core issue of low self-esteem. They focus upon the man in their thoughts and wishes. Part of the problem is that this continued focus—how great he was, what a "bastard" he was—can be an effective defense against really looking at one's personal feeling of self-worth and confidence.

For many women, it is far easier to rail about that man than to face the real problem—that they don't feel good about themselves. In our experience, we haven't seen one woman with good, solid self-esteem who became trapped in an endless state of mourning. Women with this pattern all have problems with feelings of low self-worth.

The issue, then, is not the man, but personal value. Certainly if there was validity to the reasons for rejection, these factors need to be worked on. But remember, whatever good and wholesome qualities the relationship possessed were a joint creation, and the dismantling was likewise a shared responsibility. Fault, like creation, is a joint venture.

Loving again requires relinquishing old hurt and anger. Deciding that men are all jerks or that none can match the former lover is an excuse, to prevent risk and personal exposure.

It is important for a woman to entertain the belief that she *can* love again and feel wonderful with a man not yet met, one who may be very different from the one for whom she grieves. It is important that this new, unmet man be given a chance, for he may provide an even richer experience than before. This requires much more than mere dating. It requires being open to new experiences, and it requires seeing a new man in fresh rather than comparative terms.

We are all just human beings. No one has magic. There isn't only one "right" person; there are many right people. If a woman lived in San Diego, she could find someone. If she lived in Boston, she could also find someone. It is more than possible for a woman to form a strong, meaningful, and intense relationship with someone new. But only by bolstering her self-esteem—through friends, activities, accomplishments. A renewed sense of personal worth makes it possible to generate the courage, freedom, and openness necessary to love again.

CHAPTER NINE

Freedom from Love Obsessions

The desire for a relationship with the opposite sex is a primitive and compelling magnet drawing us inexorably toward one another. In spite of pain, frustration, or failure, we somehow manage to dust ourselves off and take yet one more try for the brass ring—a lasting love.

We all seek safe harbor and nurturance in a relationship, as well as relief from loneliness, a sense of continuity, and common vision. But for some women, bonding takes on still additional meaning—the sweet agony of longing, adventure, and personal validation. For many such women, choosing a mate is related less to a selective gathering of the above ingredients and more to finding a solution to flagging self-esteem.

Men, too, are subject to self-defeating solutions to questions of core value, but they take a different form. While some women search for their "Prince" and impossibly romanticize and idealize relationships, many men are hopelessly driven by money. Money, and the symbols it buys, becomes for men a means by which to bolster their own sense of personal worth and esteem. Men plunge ahead drawn by the hope that money will infuse in them a sense of value and confidence.

Unfortunately, or perhaps fortunately depending upon your point of view, these external strategies to solve internal dilemmas don't work. Personal validation is simply more complex than that. It requires real individual accomplishment and an honest feeling of pride in one's conduct. Who we have on our arm or what we have in our wallet is not enough.

While men march on, obsessed with creating a yet larger total in their net-worth column, women too frequently fall prey to love and romance. Rather than enjoying the simple elements relationships can realistically provide, some women become obsessed with the heady thrill of challenge involved in romantic encounters.

Four Types of Love Addicts

Needing love and rating it important as an ongoing experience in life is not love addiction. Love addiction differs from normal, healthy desire when the accompanying feelings are greatly exaggerated, distorted, and fleeting. The quest for love becomes obsession.

Who is the love addict? She lives and breathes the fantasy of finding the man who will make her whole, who will provide everything that is lacking in her life. No matter what her life is like—whether she has a job she enjoys, friendships, talents, or accomplishments—she feels that nothing matters as much as romance. Every day and night without a lover she spends waiting, longing for that magical meeting.

Perhaps the most unmistakable characteristic of the love addict is her compulsion to repeat and repeat again the same pattern. It is this endless repetition that makes love addiction so destructive. The love addict sincerely believes she wants a lasting relationship with a man when in fact she really does not.

There are four basic types of love addictions, all triggered by faulty or incomplete early learning experiences, which are compounded by today's confusions regarding relationships.

HOOKED ON LONGING ■ Early in life, men and women come to associate a specific feeling with the word *love*. The definitions of love that they form are very personal and very specific to each of them. If the love provided a child by her parents is warm, giving, and consistent, the child's definition of love will reflect that contentment and become stamped firmly in place. In essence, the child learns, "I feel love when I am nurtured, when I have someone."

Many other children, conversely, experience parental love that is inconsistent, conditional, and unpredictable. That child yearns for her parents' love—longs for it. As discussed earlier, it is precisely this experience of "longing" that sometimes becomes the child's primitive concept of love. This definition says, "I feel love when I want someone." When this child becomes an adult, she continues to confuse love and longing, and the pattern becomes hunt, conquer, discard. She feels love only during the initial uncommitted phase of a relationship. Once she is certain of a man's love, she quickly loses interest. For this woman, love is not having, but wanting—which only leaves her an endless and tiring string of new conquests.

HOOKED ON VALIDATION ■ Early in life, all children look to parents for approval and validation of their worth. Good parenting gradually encourages children to think and evaluate for themselves. It is through the growing trust in their own perceptions and evaluations that they learn to like themselves and to value that judgment.

But many parents don't teach this process very well, and some children don't learn it very well. Basically, the process of self-approval involves a gradual shift and transfer of power from the parents to the child. "It's not so important what I think. What do you think? How do you feel about it?" This statement from a parent allows the child to begin to feel that she is important, that how she thinks or feels about an issue or event is of value.

Some parents instead discourage this process of self-approval by communicating to the child that it is only the parents' thoughts and attitudes that are valid. This parent may sense a loss associated with this transfer of power and enjoy keeping the child tied closely to him or her as a continuing primary source of approval. Sadly, this child is taught to look solely to others for feelings of self-worth and acceptance. As a child, this kind of girl can't look in the mirror and say, "I like what I see!" Years later, this woman looks in the mirror and wonders, "Will he like what he sees?"

An inability to validate oneself leads to serious doubts and questions about self-worth. And when you can't trust yourself you usually have the feeling that you can't trust anyone. If you don't believe you are lovable, no one can tell you that you are, no matter how many people try or how hard they try.

It is this disbelief that causes the restless repetitions for the love addict. Even when she has a man telling her that she is terrific and he loves her, she doesn't believe it. She doesn't believe it because she has never learned how to feel it herself—coming from inside herself. She is doomed to keep looking for someone else to provide the feeling of lovability.

HOOKED ON ILLUSION ■ Some women's early experiences taught them that they were vulnerable, incomplete, or worthless as separate individuals. These women were taught insecurity. They were also taught that a man was the answer to that insecurity.

You may have heard the phrase "Women are, men do." Too often, women learned that relationships meant merging with a man—finding that necessary component of autonomy, action, and protection externally, in a man.

These issues have in recent years been challenged by women. Increasingly, they are looking more to themselves for a sense of worth. Penelope Russianoff in the book *Why Do I Think I'm Nothing Without a Man?* poignantly describes the anguish and emptiness women frequently feel when there is no man around to care for them, to validate them and make them feel whole through that caring.

Many women have been taught that they need men—not because life is more pleasant when one is in their life, but as a symbol of their value as women. One woman vividly recalled her mother's typical response to a question: "Don't ask dumb old me, wait until your father gets home and ask him." In her adult relationships with men, deepseated feelings of insecurity kept emerging, feelings that she mistakenly believed a man had the power to make disappear.

This love addict is hooked on the illusion of finding that perfect man to make her feel whole and safe. Painfully aware of her insecurity, she moves from one man to the next, believing it is only a matter of time until she finds the right one.

HOOKED ON ROMANCE ■ This woman is in love with romance, infatuated with infatuation. She tells the new man in her life that she cares for him, and she truly believes she does. But like the male "rat" described earlier, she is not actually in love with the man but with the rush of new love.

As this exquisite high begins to wear off,

which it inevitably does when people get to know each other, she feels let down, disappointed, cheated. Instead of viewing this transformation of emotion as a natural phase in the evolution of love, she decides that something must be wrong—either with her capacity to care, which is too scary a thought to consider, or with him, a flaw she hadn't noticed in the beginning.

When Pat met Jerry, she knew this was "it." There had been other "its" in the past, relationships that had all fizzled, but Jerry was different. She couldn't remember feeling this strongly about a man before. This time, she knew it was going to work. Jerry knew how to make her feel wanted and womanly. As Pat recalls, "He was so expressive—much more so than most other men. He did all those nice things, like bringing me flowers—he even used to write me poems. I know it sounds corny, but it felt good." But after a couple of months, as the flush of newness faded, Pat began to have gnawing doubts and feelings of disappointment. What was, in fact, simply the end of infatuation she mistook for the end of love—again. "I guess as we got to know each other better he relaxed a bit—the poems became fewer, and instead of candles, a bottle of wine, and an intimate dinner, Jerry was just as likely to suggest catching a ball game on TV." The minor flaws which she once thought made Jerry all the more charming and endearing now became monstrously magnified in her eyes, and she felt herself slowly but surely losing her feelings for him.

When Love Becomes Obsession

Any time we experience something pleasurable we want that experience again. We develop a liking, yearning, even a craving for that feeling. This is true for all of us. But if we are sufficiently varied and well rounded in our tastes and desires, we don't become fixated on one activity. Healthy people tend to seek balance and variety in life. Others develop an overwhelming or repetitive compulsion for that one special or intoxicating experience. This need can become so powerful that it persists in spite of the negative physical or emotional consequences of satisfying it. Addicted people are willing to endure anything in order to reexperience that physical and psychological state of being, that compelling satisfaction they feel whenever they take in that substance, whatever it is—alcohol, drugs, nicotine, food, or a man's love. This hunger for love becomes obsession when it reaches such a proportion that the woman feels she needs it just to feel that life is worth living, just to maintain her everyday emotional balance.

From the time she was a child, Jessica was taught that men were of paramount importance in her life. She was never encouraged to have girlfriends, for they were seen as frivolous and of little real use. She had boyfriends beginning in her early teen years, and with each one she lived in dread of his breaking up with her. Jessica's parents always sided with the boys and would grill her about what she had "done wrong."

Jessica's mother also placed major importance on Jessica's looks: her clothes, hair, grooming, and weight. "You want to be popular, don't you?" Using those words as well as the unspoken giving and withholding of approval, her parents slowly taught Jessica to distrust and undervalue her own sense of self and to defer to the wishes and demands of men.

Her parents made it clear that she would be nothing without a man. Jessica exhibits one of the crucial, telltale signs of love addiction: She feels worthless and incomplete without a man. Needing love is normal and natural. Feeling worthless, empty, and desperate without it is not.

Angela, a 28-year-old physical therapist, didn't regard herself as a love addict, but she displayed one of the sure signs. Whenever she had plans with a woman friend and a man called to ask her out at the last minute, she would change her plans. Angela felt no guilt about this. "Well, you'd do it too, wouldn't you?" she would ask her girlfriends. No, as it turned out, most of them would not. Angela lost several good friends as a direct result of her continued habit of breaking dates with them. After one of her closest girlfriends refused to speak to her for months for doing this, Angela told another friend, "As much as I hate to admit it, a date with a man is more important to me than just going somewhere with a girlfriend. I can't help feeling like that—I don't want to miss out on a chance for attention from a man."

An obsession is a habit which eventually begins to influence daily existence. Love addicts are people who feel they can't live without the person who nourishes them. Even the mere anticipation of the longed-for experience can be the source of a kind of pleasure. The love addict thus becomes hooked by the process of "looking-for-love." It is as though the experience of "looking forward to" itself takes on the power to satisfy.

Sheila, a 41-year-old computer programmer, dates frenetically. Before each date she loses her appetite and blames it on being "too excited." It is as though the anticipation of being satisfied by a man is itself filling enough. Many love addicts have this sensation; the excitement of anticipation can, in and of itself, serve as a temporary pacifier.

In the beginning phase of love addiction, women are convinced that the excitement they experience with men is the reason why they continue the behavior. But in the later phases, even the love addict admits she is hooked. Few are actually aware of the lack of pleasure in their repetitive experiences. Love addicts insist they enjoy chasing after men even when it's obvious to everyone around them that they are miserable.

The core satisfaction of love addiction is not so much the particular pleasure experienced with a specific man, but the escape provided from daily anxiety or frustration. Love addicts are most frequently women for whom the world seems bleak, empty, and fraught with perils. As noted earlier, love addictions represent poorly understood attempts by women to solve problems of self-worth, completion, and personal validation. Relief from these deep feelings of insecurity is found in the thoughts, feelings, and fantasies these women have about men. This "relief," however, is both fleeting and illusory and exists only as a temporary state of excitement and promise of contentment. What better feeling than the euphoria of falling in love?

The prospect of a new romance can be totally energizing. Catherine, a 29-year-old court reporter, spends many of her evenings with friends at singles bars and invariably finds herself going home with a man she barely knows. She covers up a vague discomfort with her own conduct by viewing herself as being free to experiment with men. "It's just a game to me, to see which guy I can land for the evening." However, when pressed, Catherine admits she feels driven to these nightly interludes. It is not really so much the sex she enjoys, she says, as it is the chase and the illusion of being attractive and popular. Catherine is not a sex addict, she is a love addict, for without this compulsive activity she feels empty and depressed more often than not.

Men who engage in a frantic searching for relatively meaningless sexual encounters are said to suffer from a Don Juan complex. But for both male and female, the core problem is the same. Love addiction is a futile and self-destructive way to feel filled up, to create an illusion of love and emotional nourishment.

Most addictions are difficult to break—particularly those which appear relatively harmless. On the surface, the love addict can seem highly successful with men, and her friends may actually be jealous of her romantic and sexual triumphs.

Time *Is* Running Out

When Ellen, a 38-year-old book editor, finally decided to try to overcome her love addiction, she initially experienced an overwhelming sense of relief. Her entire adulthood, from 21 to 38, had been a series of tumultuous love affairs, with two brief marriages thrown in as seeming statements of her capacity for commitment and stability. She was highly involved in her work, but her real thrills came from her relationships with men. Ellen is witty and vivacious, and had had no difficulty attracting men. But each of her relationships lasted a few months and typically ended with her loss of interest and the quick conversion of romance into friendship.

She secretly knew her days were framed by dreams of her next lover and whether "he" would be the one who could sustain the intensity of her "high." Secretly, she was becoming increasingly tired of the "blahs" she felt at the end of each relationship.

When she decided to take a break from the merry-go-round, it was with a great sigh of relief. But, after a month of abstinence she discovered something terrifying. It slowly dawned on her that life felt meaningless a good deal of the time. More precisely, except for those romantic thrills, she had no ability to really savor many of the experiences she thought she enjoyed. Going to a ballet meant nothing unless her latest infatuation was by her side. Her friends bored her when they weren't talking about men. She even became emotionally detached from her work. She realized that her editor's job meant less to her when she wasn't communicating her work to a man.

Ellen was frightened by the powerful feelings beneath her love addiction. But she now had to deal with them, because something happened to her that happens to a lot of women when they reach their late thirties. She realized how much she wanted to have children and that time was running out.

Women have quite a different sense of time than do men. For men, time is often a dimension by which they measure their progress toward career success. Women also experience time in that way. But unlike men, virtually all women are extremely sensitive to the ticking of the biological clock against which they measure the passage of their reproductive years.

A woman is reminded of this every month. If she has no children, is not married, and is in her early thirties, she feels the inexorable pressure of time if she wants to become a mother. Women are fortunate in this regard, because this pressure compels them to confront self-defeating behavior patterns if their goal is to marry and have children.

Susie was 33 years old when her last brief relationship fizzled out. At the same time her best friend, who had recently married, announced her pregnancy. The combination of these two events had a profound effect on Susie. She was envious of her friend and had a nagging uneasiness about her own romantic history and decisions with men. She knew that if she was ever going to consider marriage seriously, she would have to take a good look at the string of men she had rejected. "It was scary because I knew in that bunch there must have been someone who should have worked out." When she went out shopping or to the beach or the park, she found herself looking at young mothers and families instead of men. She was beginning to feel that she was losing out on something far more important than romantic flings, and this growing awareness saddened her. She was feeling melancholy in a way she never had before.

Vicki, a 43-year-old film studio executive, had given up on children; nevertheless, she still worried about the passage of time. She had had many lovers, both married and single. But she, too, yearned for a more quiet and settled life—to fill the need she had for things her professional success could not give her.

All of these women felt pressured by their biological clocks to reassess their patterns of involvement with men. They gradually came to realize that what they had been seeking was the exciting, elusive relationship that gave them only a brief high or infatuation, and that they tended to overlook genuinely positive qualities in men. Susie recalled how annoyed she was when a friend commented about the man with whom she had just broken up, "You know, John is really a great guy, but you're never satisfied. You're always looking for something you don't have." Fortunately, Susie was smart enough to realize that she wouldn't have gotten so irritated if her friend's remarks hadn't hit close to home.

Getting Excitement Elsewhere

Love addicts, like other addicts, panic and feel depressed and empty at the thought of giving up their cravings. Because of this, the optimum time for a woman to consider change is when she becomes bored or disgusted with her addiction. Only then is change possible.

The more restricted a woman's sources of excitement and satisfaction are, the greater the chances that she will become highly attached to one of them. As noted earlier, women traditionally have been programmed to look for sources of excitement, fulfillment, and validation in the context of relationships. To overcome love addiction, it is necessary to seek exhilaration and enhancements to personal identity elsewhere.

Finding a substitute object for this craving is not easy. There is probably no more wonderfully exciting experience than that of falling in love—again and again and again. But there are other kinds of experience that can be equally pleasurable—spending more time with women friends, for example. It can be rewarding if the conversations revolve around subjects other than men. But even if it's talk about men, it's often fun—especially if you're honest.

Cindy tried this. After many years of making men the central focus in her life, she decided to try abstinence for a while. "I found that even when a bunch of us women went out for drinks and we started griping about the men we knew, it was fun because we were very honest, and we started to talk about how much we relied on men to make us feel good, and how absurd that was. Suddenly everything was in perspective." Even though Cindy had many women friends, she discovered how little time she had actually spent with them. She was able to rediscover how valuable friendship is and how much women have to offer one another.

The simple process of sharing thoughts with people who struggle with the same issues has a cleansing effect. In this way it is possible for a woman to see her own fears with greater perspective and see how self-defeating some of her behavior may be. One of the benefits of the women's movement was discovering this sense of sisterhood and common experience.

It can also be helpful for a woman to closely examine the activities she enjoys and the places she likes to go. Women often have a tendency to see the activities they shared with men they dated—attending plays, concerts, lectures, sports events—as activities that can only be enjoyed with a man, not by themselves.

One woman poignantly described this common dilemma: "I always thought I was pretty sophisticated. I felt as comfortable going to the opera as I did to the movies, enjoyed the finest restaurants, art openings, and museums. It wasn't until I really stopped to think that I realized I thought of all these things as something to do with a man, never alone. It had been years since I had walked into a movie theater alone or had eaten dinner in a restaurant by myself. I literally had to force myself to do it. I can't remember ever feeling so self-conscious. I felt everyone was looking at me, even though I knew no one was."

Even though some women still think of work or career as something worth pursuing only until they get married and have children, the truth is that professional accomplishment can be an important source of excitement and gratification. No one achieves full satisfaction in life without committing to some major involvement that requires either creative expression, mastery, or achievement. By "major" we mean something beyond the hobby or dabbling level. This doesn't mean a woman must get paid for this work or that her friends must approve of it. But it does mean that she needs to throw herself into it wholeheartedly and develop personal goals which will enable her to experience the excitement and rewards of progress. This doesn't preclude occasional failure, though; for it is only through occasional failure that we know we are taking risks and therefore making progress.

Breaking Old Patterns
Can Be Exciting

There is probably nothing more difficult for an adult to do than change. A lot of us are dissatisfied and want to change one aspect of our lives or another, but few of us actually accomplish this goal. Why? Change requires a willingness to face the unknown, and the unknown is always frightening. It's easier to stick with what's familiar and "feels" safe. Change also requires adopting new modes of behavior, which are always uncomfortable in the beginning. Often it isn't until people become extremely frightened, disgusted, or angry about their own behavior that they can summon enough motivation to carry them through those initial stages of discomfort.

Evelyn was in her late thirties before she became sufficiently miserable about her love addiction. She had been in therapy three different times since the age of 24, each time for at least one year. She explains, "I really thought I was working at it. I mean it! I felt I made a lot of progress and I was going to change the way I picked men and the feeling of panic I had to hook up with someone. Only this last time did I realize how much I was kidding myself.

"It was as if I found a new game to play. Every time I broke up with a man, I would find a male therapist and we would explore who I was without a man. I thought I was sincere, but I recognize now that I was very dishonest. It reminded me of planning to quit smoking—all the talk is easy, but the doing it is really tough."

One effective way of changing behavior is to try to find the process of change itself exciting —in other words, rather than seeing change merely as a means to an end, seeing the *process* of change as a new challenge. Although change is never easy, it can be challenging, stimulating, and, of course, ultimately rewarding. One tactic for making change interesting and less serious is to view life as a series of strategies or games and change simply as a process of switching from an old game to a new one.

Mercedes, a 34-year-old travel agent, had little success overcoming her destructive love addiction until she consulted a therapist who forbade her to talk at all of men during session. Instead, he said, she was to talk only of different experiences she found joyful and pleasurable. Her homework was to seek out those experiences and rewards separate from interaction with men.

At first, Mercedes resisted this tactic. Gradually, however, she began rediscovering the delights of visiting museums, relearning to ice skate, training for a bicycle race, going on Sierra Club hikes, spending time with friends—all the interests which, in her single-minded focus on men, she had long neglected.

The most powerful reward for change, of course, is the elimination of pain. Love addicts, as we have noted, tend to ignore the pain of their self-defeating behavior and concentrate instead on the immediate pleasure—the thrill or the high. In order to change, they must first confront the self-defeating aspects of their behavior. They must then be willing to forgo short-term thrills in favor of the long-term satisfactions that come from putting an end to a frustrating and repetitious behavior pattern.

The satisfaction of experiencing change—the heightened awareness of "will," self-mastery, and personal power—can be wonderfully reinforcing. Change leads to a new, more positive definition of the self and to a growing sense of being in better control. The more a woman cares and respects herself, the less compelled she is to seek validation or completion from a relationship with a man.

Ultimately, the cure for love obsessions is to develop personal acceptance and wholeness. We all deserve to believe that we are all right just being who we are—with or without a lover or mate.

CHAPTER TEN

Letting Go of Expectations

E xpectations are not simply predictions of what will happen to us, but what we want to happen. We all have expectations, for they are a natural outgrowth of customs, roles, and, more important, personal needs.

If what we expect in a relationship is what we actually experience, there is usually no problem. Unfortunately, that doesn't happen very often, for most frequently, there is a discrepancy between expectation and real experience —we expect one thing but get another. Expectations in any relationship present potential problems, for if they are not met, they are accompanied by feelings of disappointment. Today, during this time of social change and role redefinition, expectations in a man/woman relationship are especially tricky.

Hidden Agendas

It's eight in the evening, and you're racing to finish putting on your makeup. You've waited all week for this moment. A good friend has fixed you up with someone who sounds terrific. It's been quite a while since you've been this excited about a date, but this man sounds different ... special. The doorbell rings. You draw a deep breath, calm down enough to assume a casual pose, and open the door.

In those first few seconds, you will check each other out, resulting in a multitude of impressions. These initial impressions will be stimulated by physical likes and dislikes. As the evening progresses, other impressions begin to form, and the picture gets increasingly complex. We all want to make a good impression and be found attractive, bright, and enjoyable to be with. But in addition to these immediate concerns, there are also powerful hopes and desires at work beneath our conscious thoughts —hopes about the kind of person we want or need, hopes about the kind of life we wish to share with him, and fantasies about love, fulfillment, ecstasy, romance. These deeper desires are like shadowy companions that can accompany a woman on a date, desires which her escort may sense subliminally.

Occasionally, a woman may feel vaguely uncomfortable about an encounter with a man, even though on the surface everything seemed to go just fine. This is usually because of a variety of needs and expectations that are not being directly communicated. She may have a "hidden agenda" within herself that she is unaware of.

Claire, a 29-year-old investment banker, described some recent changes in how she feels about men. "I went through a long period in which I didn't have a relationship with a man that lasted any more than a couple of weeks. I knew I was pushing too hard, trying to make things happen too fast. I'm not sure where I learned it, but I had this wild, romantic fantasy in my head about what the man would be like and how things were supposed to happen. When it didn't, I tried to make it happen.

"I used to pray every day to be relieved of that terrible romantic obsession. Finally, out of utter frustration, I gave it up, knowing it just wasn't meant to be. When I was with a man, I focused on trying to find out who he was, not how I wanted him to be. It was amazing! I found I actually enjoyed men in a way I never had before."

Many men sense what a woman feels or needs from them even when it is not put into words. In fact, when a woman's expectations are non-verbal, they can have an even more powerful effect upon a man.

Jim, a 39-year-old real estate agent, sadly described his intentions to break off a relationship with a nice, attractive woman he had been seeing for several weeks. He thought his decision was only another example of his general discomfort with women, but in session it was revealed that certain feelings on the woman's part had triggered his fear.

Joan, a stockbroker in her early thirties, tried to build him up every time he was down or frustrated about his work. Rather than letting him express his discouragement, she would immediately interject that he was terrific, that things would work out, that he would "pull it out of the ditch." While this was done in the spirit of help and encouragement, in fact, it had the effect of inhibiting communication. His frustration built. When he tried to talk to her, she admitted that it made her anxious to see him in such an insecure state. She didn't know how to respond to his anxiety. What she really wanted to do was to make it go away, for its presence made her feel insecure. This woman basically wants a man to be strong and confident. Jim too would like to be that kind of man and has that potential. But in order to feel comfortable with a woman he must also be able to express feelings of doubt or insecurity without fear of judgment.

Not all expressions of women's expectations are of a verbal nature. Often our body language describes what we want or what we fear. These feelings are revealed in the way we walk, talk, move, when we touch, who initiates affection, and so on.

Alex is a recently divorced attorney in his early thirties. His ex-wife was cold and rejecting for many reasons, some of which had to do with Alex's neglect of her when he was struggling through law school. Alex had been dating only a short time when he met Jeannie, a woman he liked right away. She was fun to talk to, and they were easy and relaxed with each other right from the beginning.

By the third date, they found themselves necking on the couch of her apartment. But when it came to sex, she was extremely shy, almost to the point of appearing frozen. It reminded him of high school, when "nice girls" had to hide their passion behind a mask of modesty to such an extreme that they appeared uninterested in sex.

Alex tried to tell himself that she was only

shy and nervous, but her sudden lack of eye contact and her physical reserve unnerved him. In retrospect, he was aware that every move had been initiated by him. She expected him to take the lead, be the aggressor. While this was acceptable to him up to a point, he also found her passivity to be scary. Most men enjoy being the aggressor, but extreme female passivity becomes unattractive, for men associate it with a lack of interest or passion. Men are no different from women—they need to feel wanted and desired.

Another expectation women have that affects men concerns commitment. Many women believe that men fundamentally don't want to commit to long-term relationships or marriage. To the contrary, most single men are actually looking for a woman to get involved with and marry. And they do. When men fall in love, they fall hard and quickly, and often for the first women for whom they feel a great deal of trust.

Janet, a 41-year-old social worker, believes men are fundamentally afraid of intimacy, and she carries this expectation along with her on every date. The men she goes out with sense her hopes for love as well as the bitterness and cynicism that surround and protect these hopes. Such conflicting emotions are confusing, for they are a reaction to men in general rather than a response to individuals. Her hunger and old anger combine in such a way that invariably these men end up fulfilling her prophecy.

Most women between the ages of 25 and 45 have one foot planted in traditional roles and are gingerly probing new territory with the other. The result is often a set of confusing and contradictory feelings. Such women seem to be looking for a man who is vulnerable but strong, communicative but self-contained, sensitive yet aggressive and protective. It would be wonderful if there were an abundant supply of men who possessed this combination of qualities, but unfortunately there is not. It is perhaps a cruel paradox that most men who are vulnerable, communicative, and sensitive are not those whom women typically see as strong, aggressive, and self-contained.

Faced with these mixed messages from women, men become nervous, unsure, even distrustful—they don't know which message to believe. Says one man about the young woman with whom he is involved, "I don't know what she wants from me. She says she wants to know all about me. But when I finally did confide some of my insecurities, it was like my worst nightmare come true. I could see by the look on her face that she thought less of me."

Even many economically self-sufficient

women also secretly expect a potential mate to be able to take care of them financially. As Rick put it, "The more successful the woman, the more exaggerated her wishes for the Prince." Rick, a 43-year-old doctor, was dating the female vice-president of marketing for a large corporation. He found her to be bright and aggressive and was excited about the relationship until they finally decided to take a trip to Tahiti. They earned roughly the same amount of money, but when Rick mentioned that he expected her to pay for her own tickets, she was surprised. It wasn't that she couldn't afford the air fare. But it just didn't feel right. It made her feel less womanly and caused her to see him as less manly. She knew what she was saying didn't make much sense, but it was how she felt.

Many women are embarrassed by such desires as wanting the man to "take care of" all the expenses, for those wishes run counter to their belief in equality. They "think" equality, but for many there is a simultaneous tug from the past deep inside that feels quite different. And no matter how diligently a woman attempts to deny or hide such secret expectations about men, they manage to find expression.

Expectations about control in a relationship can also play havoc when they are hidden. Some women will go to great lengths to have their way, and yet be dismayed when they get it. Laurel, a successful 42-year-old antique dealer, is currently involved with Mickey, an equally successful and amiable CPA. Most of their social life revolves around her friends and the things she likes to do. Mickey is happy to go along with her suggestions, and he actually believes he's pleasing her. Laurel knows his love for her is such that she can say or do just about anything without jeopardizing the relationship.

Instead of feeling happy and secure, Laurel feels bored and too safe. Secretly, Laurel thinks Mickey is wishywashy. She can't trust a man who bends so easily or is influenced by her desires. She wants a man to be strong, powerful, and in charge. Yet Laurel stays, feeling dissatisfied, and Mickey feels a growing resentment over the lack of respect he senses from her.

Hidden expectations diminish warmth and honesty and prevent people from being free and natural with each other. They put a damper on fresh and novel exchanges between the sexes.

Expectations Versus Intimacy

Joan, a 43-year-old foundation administrator, has been divorced for four years. Immediately following the divorce she spent a great deal of time with her woman friends. The occasional man in her life never seemed to match the warmth and variety of interest she found in her friends, and these men were discarded one by one. She had been married to a dedicated doctor and saw men in much the same way she used to see her ex-husband—"into their work and their sports."

It was not until a close friend pointed out her attitude to her that Joan saw how she categorized men and how rigid her expectations were. As she saw this self-defeating cycle, Joan began to develop a more open and fresh response to men. Much to her surprise, she became aware that changes in her attitudes had the positive effect of allowing men to feel more comfortable, relaxed, and expressive with her.

Men and women are in the midst of a transition, shifting away from traditional sex roles and discovering new ones—the result being that their expectations of each other have become ambiguous and confused. This is unfortunate, because if there is one simple truth, it is that the greater the number of expectations, the less likely it is that the relationship will prosper.

To maximize the probability that a relationship will take root, it is imperative that a man and woman be open and self-revealing—no disguises and as few filters as possible. When either person's behavior is dictated by preconceived notions or expectations, personal expressiveness is reduced, severely limiting the possibility of genuine intimacy.

Single people complain, for example, about the predictable quality of the first encounter. "Nothing feels fresh anymore." They explain that the opening lines, the topics raised, even the jokes at singles bars and other singles meeting places are stale and boring. The real problem, of course, is that people are afraid to let go and be themselves. In another setting, where they felt more comfortable and open, these same people might prove to be much more interesting.

The men and women who complain most loudly might also want to contemplate the nature of the self-fulfilling prophecy: When either a man or a woman anticipates boredom, it will probably be found. Perhaps the woman adopts the pose of the aloof observer. The man, in turn, falls back on a predictable conversational pattern. Neither allows enough room, or makes enough effort, for the unexpected or new to occur. The freer men and women allow themselves to be, the more likely they are to connect in a new way.

The important thing for women to remember is that expectation is the enemy of intimacy. The more a man feels pressured to live up to a woman's expectations, the less likely he is to relax and open up. Men, like women, want to be accepted for who they are, rather than be expected to become what someone else wants or needs them to be.

Getting in Touch with Hidden Illusions

The wish to remake or change someone so that he is a bit more to our liking is as futile as it is common. There are no perfect matches, and difficult as it may seem at times, it is far easier to find someone you like and respect than to try to create that person.

Adrianne, a 37-year-old sales representative, said, "I finally think I've learned my lesson. If I realize that there's something I really dislike or can't respect in a man, I move on, but the little things I'm learning to overlook. In the past, I always seemed to be drawn to guys who had problems, and I mean big ones. You'd think that would have scared me away, but it didn't. I remember thinking that my love would help or do something positive for these men. Well, I never changed anybody, and I know now that I can't. Now I'm with a man I really like. Oh, he's got his quirks and his moods, but I leave them alone. I actually feel freer not having to change or do something about them."

Some women find it easier to adopt a passive, "wishing" attitude, rather than to deal with cold, hard reality. They become involved with a man, thinking, "He'll change," or, worse, "Someday I'll change him." More likely, these unspoken needs will cloud and confuse communication. The only way to clear it up is through straight talk. And this kind of direct communication takes effort and practice. It requires that a woman tell a man what she secretly expects and find out from him how many of these expectations he is willing or able to satisfy.

Melissa, although she didn't realize it, wanted her man to be the strong and decisive one in the relationship. Yet at the same time, she wanted him to respect her and be sensitive to her wishes. When she and Chuck moved in together and were decorating their apartment, they found themselves fighting almost constantly. Chuck wanted to discuss every decision with her. She had certain ideas, yet she wanted him to ultimately make the decisions, partly because it was his money and partly because she secretly wanted a more fatherly kind of mate who would take charge.

One day, she discussed her battles with a

friend, who pointed out to Melissa that she hated having so much control. Why not tell Chuck? Melissa didn't want to do this, because she felt that if she told him, he would just be taking over to please her, and not because he was really stronger. Her friend rightly pointed out that Chuck's wish to please came out of love and not weakness.

Sometimes a woman resists verbalizing her desires out of a misguided belief that she shouldn't have to tell a man what she wants— that if he really loved her, he would know. Or perhaps she worries that if a man does then try to satisfy her desires, he will be doing so begrudgingly.

She may fear that her mate will prove unwilling, or unable, to meet those expectations. Perhaps he can. Perhaps he can't. She may be given more than she ever hoped for. Or she may realize that her needs are never going to be met and decide to end the relationship. Either way, she will at least have a more realistic sense of the relationship's potential. And reality is ultimately much more satisfying than illusion.

Some women find it helpful to discuss their hidden expectations with female or male friends who know them well and can be objective. And of course, if a woman is in a long-term relationship, she should discuss them with her partner. Many women balk at this suggestion, but that's foolish. While it's difficult to do, a woman can save herself a lot of time and grief. The discovery of hidden attitudes and wishes that push men away makes change possible and frees a woman and the man she is with or wants to be with to explore each other in fresh new ways.

Expectations That Work

Obviously, not all expectations are bad or destructive to a relationship. Some are positive and can enhance feelings of comfort and closeness with a man.

Expectations, to a great extent, grow out of the ways in which we view and value ourselves. If we think poorly of ourselves, expectations typically assume a distinctly negative cast. If we relate to ourselves positively, expectations then flow in that direction—we expect what we feel we deserve and we get what we expect.

It is easy to see, then, how important it is first to trust in our basic values and worth in a relationship and second to assume our partner will also see and appreciate who we are.

A woman who expects men to be insensitive, unloving, or untrustworthy frequently finds just that. A woman who expects men to be sensitive to her, who assumes, until it is proved otherwise, they can be trusted, and who expects a man will want to love and commit himself to her can also find that actually happening. This is no accident. Positive expectations allow the man to sense value in himself, for they assume he is capable of fulfilling them. Such expectations give a man something to live up to; they establish a model for personal conduct. When you expect sensitivity and gentleness from a man, expect him to respect you and not to betray your trust, expect him to be good and loving—there is a far greater chance that he will be.

CHAPTER ELEVEN

Finding Diamonds
in the Rough

The first date was going disastrously. Ned had fumbled his way through before-dinner drinks, he had spilled pumpkin soup on his tie, and now there was a sheen of perspiration on his balding scalp. His date was looking intently at her nails, cursing the "best friend" who had set them up. When Ned's beeper went off, both of them jumped in relief. This date was going nowhere.

Ned did one smart thing that night. He asked his date to go along on the call. Ned is one of the few pediatricians who still makes house calls. What his date found out that night couldn't have been discovered in a month of dinners in dimly lit restaurants.

The contrast was remarkable. The man who hadn't been sure what to order at dinner was now absolutely confident in the presence of his young patient. He reassured, coaxed, entertained, and probed to get his job done. It was a poignant time, because the child had been in great pain.

Slowly, Ned's date began to see him in an entirely different light. At the restaurant, she had been sure he was a loser—average-looking without any real style, painfully shy and anxious. Even though she'd been encouraged by the "best friend" to take the time to get to know Ned, she knew she would never agree to a second date. Before his beeper went off, she had been trying to figure out a way to get him to take her home directly after dinner.

After the house call, they went to an all-night diner for coffee. What she had seen allowed her to focus on Ned's passion, the kids he takes care of, the commitment he feels to helping people. It suddenly wasn't as important anymore that Ned was shy or clumsy at first glance.

There are a lot of men who may not fit the mold that many women have when it comes to "Mr. Right"—men who may have visible flaws in behavior or appearance, men who may be insecure when it comes to initially forming relationships. They may not have "the look," they may be awkward conversationalists. Worst of all, they may be too available, too eager. But these are often men who possess great possibilities. They truly are "diamonds in the rough."

Amy is a 36-year-old buyer for a department store. She's brunette, athletic, and very aggressive. She believes she deserves someone who is terrific, and, of course, she does. A friend had fixed her up with Robert.

"I told Louise over lunch that even though he had called for a second date, I didn't plan to see him again. I made up some flimsy story about why, because I knew he was an old friend of hers and I didn't want to hurt her feelings. Well, she immediately saw through my story and really nailed me. What she said wasn't something I didn't already know, but I hadn't heard someone put it into those words before. She said, 'I know why you don't want to see Robert again. He doesn't quite measure up to your standards—good looks, easy talker, confident, and a rat. Let me tell you something about Robert. He's a little shy, but when you get beyond that, he is one of the brightest and funniest men I know. He isn't the athletic type you're attracted to, but he's warm, interesting, and serious about wanting to be in a relationship. All I can tell you is that you're missing out on something very special. The men you go for all get worse as you get to know them.

Robert is the kind of man who gets better and better.' "

Some men don't show well. Some of them, like Chris, just don't care. At first glance, you'd peg him for a hick—the Texas drawl, the slicked-down hair. He is tall and dark but too rough-looking. He's been told his clothes are out of date and still he refuses to change much. Chris is not trendy. But then, that is one of his strong points.

He is an attorney in an office which has a lot of flashy, dynamic go-getters in it. Chris isn't the one who gets the most clients, but he is the one who keeps them. He is a brilliant trial lawyer who wins over juries. Out of the courtroom, he is loyal, trustworthy, patient—all qualities which are great for dogs but not so great for "Mr. Right." At least, that's what many women would think.

Chris is so secure in himself that he doesn't worry about external appearances, but it certainly diminishes his romantic chances. The woman who finally bothered to look beyond the obvious found a jewel. Chris, she found out, was strong enough to put up with most of her flaws—not because he was weak or dependent, but because he had a fundamental strength and tolerance. It is a strength she initially found boring, but now it's something she wouldn't live without.

There are a great many men, and of course women, too, who are very slow in revealing themselves. They are usually people who have experienced rejection in some form in the past and, having been once burned, are now twice shy. The smart woman should know how to get past the exterior awkwardness that many men may display.

"I wouldn't say Mitchell was boring, but he seemed so conservative," Andrea said as she leaned back in the chair. Thirty-two and an attractive blonde, she worked for the city as an administrative aide to a councilwoman. She had a penchant for high-powered political types who invariably would walk all over her before they walked out the door. She needed a change.

"Mitchell just wasn't my type. He's not fat, but his face has this chubby, sort of well-fed quality to it." Andrea always liked her men lean and mean. "It turns out he *is* well-fed. God, he's a fantastic gourmet cook. He brings the same thoroughness to cooking that he brings to everything else he does. He strikes me as the kind of man who felt homely as a child, unpopular, and tried to compensate for it in other ways.

"You know, he likes to be a winner. He tries very hard to succeed, and he does eventually because he just won't give up. That's made him a success as a computer designer and also as a piano player—he's even a good photographer. No flash there, just substance.

"It seemed strange at first that Mitchell would be ill at ease in groups, but now I understand that in order to open up, he has to feel accepted. That's just the opposite of most of the men I've gone with. When they open up, there's nothing inside. Thank God for Mitchell."

Brent was almost a dead ringer for Woody Allen. The glasses, the hesitant manner, the New York accent. He grew up in Brooklyn and spent his high school years yearning to be an athletic star. But he was a great listener. He knew all the pretty girls and all the cheerleaders. He knew more about them than any other boy, because Brent was considered "safe." He was the "best friend" of the girls, but also the last one they'd ever want for a boyfriend.

That characterization continued into adulthood. Brent was an incredibly easy person to be with for most women—attentive, confident, sweet, and nice. But there never seemed to be any passion. Brent had dated a lot of women, but invariably they became friends instead of lovers.

Diane was desperate when she called Brent. Her 4-year-old son had a raging fever and was mumbling incoherently. The call she placed to her doctor had not yet been returned, and when she called her boyfriend, he merely tried to placate her with superficial reassurances. As a single parent she worried a lot about her son, she feels maybe too much, but then she had no one else around to share her concerns.

When Diane finally decided to drive Todd to the emergency room, everything went wrong. Her car had no gas, and another frantic call to her boyfriend was met with irritation. He said she was "too hysterical, too overprotective, and too demanding." That was when she thought of Brent. They had worked together for the last year. They were warm and friendly with each other, but she had never considered him as someone she would date.

When Brent picked up the phone and heard Diane's anxious voice, he was quickly on the way to her house. He was the one who carried her feverish son into the hospital. The doctors reassured her that it was just a virus and gave her instructions for his care, and they were sent home.

Inwardly, Diane was aware of a new feeling for Brent. Even though he wasn't her "type," she had strong feelings of attraction for him. She watched the way he was with Todd and how warm and sympathetic he was to her. She admired his willingness to get involved and the calm but decisive way he handled himself. She felt secure in a way she had never felt with a man. Brent and Diane began to date and eventually became deeply involved.

Most of the time we make up our minds very quickly about people, particularly when it concerns whether or not we are attracted to them. In a brief encounter, we rely most heavily upon visual information and various other data transmitted through body language.

Most people are ruled out at this point if they don't generate some vague ephemeral "chemistry." Those who are screened out pass somewhere into the misty background. Those who are screened in are elevated to the next level of inspection; we will talk to them and see what happens.

When we first meet someone, our initial dialogue reveals more about how comfortable we are with strangers, or how glib we are, than anything of real meaning or depth. Many of the potential romantic partners we didn't reject at the visual inspection level fail at this point if we are not interested or intrigued by them. And all too often, the best men are not among those few who survive that first critical five minutes of encounter.

We all make snap judgments, and for some very good reasons. We have trained ourselves to become more and more efficient using less and less information to arrive at decisions. In most areas of life this efficiency works in our favor, but not when it comes to selecting a potential mate.

While women should certainly trust their basic "gut reactions" to a person, they should also recognize that some of the most complex, sincere, and sensitive men often do not make the best first impressions. These men are frequently ignored or rejected—not because of what they are, but because of what they aren't during those first critical moments. Some women make these decisions with frightening speed, according to superficial and incomplete data.

While not the "perfect" man (no one is), the diamond in the rough is a good deal more special than he initially appears. The kind of genuinely good man we are talking about only appears to be ordinary, which may be why women sometimes miss him.

Rachel, a 31-year-old legal secretary, almost missed out. She chased unsuccessfully after elusive, seemingly fascinating men, all the while commiserating with Freddie, a rather nondescript young attorney who invariably told her that she deserved better. They occasionally had dinner together, but she never thought of him as anything more than a good friend. Then one day she saw him joking with another secretary and suddenly realized how deep her feelings for him had become. They began to date and a year later married. Rachel admits she found a diamond in the rough; if she had not worked with him, she might never have discovered him. Ordinarily, she wouldn't have been at all attracted to a man like Freddie.

In fact, the diamond in the rough is quite special. He has developed qualities of personality and character that are more substantial than flashy. If he appears less aggressive and more sensitive than other men, it may be because he's less defensive and cocky, more comfortable with openness. He is the kind of man about whom you might say, "I feel safe and comfortable with him, but I don't know, there's just no sizzle." What some women fail to understand is that what they call "sizzle" is really nothing more than uncertainty and nervousness about their place in a man's affection. There is really nothing terrific about feeling anxious. And there is really nothing wrong with feeling safe and comfortable with a man. After all, that is what a good, stable relationship is all about.

Frequently, a woman rejects this sort of man, depreciating him because she can't discriminate between niceness and weakness. These men do not have tough exteriors, and their decision-making center has a very complex and broad base. They won't have the postures, the cocky and sometimes brittle behavior, you see in some other men. They are often more sensitive and thoughtful. But remember, their ways are forged not out of weakness but from a sense of their own strength and comfort. Such a man must be allowed to develop at his own pace. If you push him to change, it can lead to disaster.

Carrie, a 42-year-old attorney in a large Los Angeles law firm, has been married and divorced twice. Her first husband, Dave, was a student she met while they were both in law school. Dave was going to be the next Clarence Darrow, but he spent more time attending antiwar rallies than studying. She saw him as a fiery comet who needed some kind of guide through the mundane aspects of life. She would take notes for him during class while he was off on one crusade or another, and she carefully prepared him for all his exams.

They were married during their second year of law school, and he moved into her apartment. Following graduation, Carrie passed the bar and landed an excellent job. Dave failed the bar and took a job clerking for an attorney in a free legal-aid clinic. Carrie took on progressively more responsibility, and her resentment toward Dave mounted with each new burden. Dave had no motivation either to retake the bar exam or to look for the kind of high-paying job that Carrie felt he should strive for.

Carrie loved Dave's warmth and deeply respected his dedication to ideals. However, she disliked his lack of push. After years of fighting, Carrie filed for divorce.

Dave may sound like a loser, but not when you hear the postscript to this story. After the divorce, and without the pain and pressure of Carrie's disappointment in him, Dave began to grow up and find himself. He eventually became successful as a business consultant and is quite happily remarried. The lesson here? Dave was a diamond in the rough who needed time to discover his niche in life.

The Mask of Shyness

One reason women may not recognize the diamond in the rough is that his worth is frequently hidden under layers of shyness. The "nerd" at the office, the obnoxious fellow at the singles bar, and the seemingly aloof neighbor across the hall may all be men of character and substance whose shyness causes them to adopt these masks. Women sometimes forget that men have private "selves" as well as those they present in public. Men met in public may show only bits and pieces of themselves.

For example, Nelson, a 43-year-old divorced physician, is generally considered a "catch," but he can be pretty obnoxious—particularly on the first date when he is uncomfortable. On that first date, he's likely to be loud and boisterous and brag about money, possessions, vacations, and so on. Women find him insufferable. What they don't know is that in spite of outward appearance, Nelson has always been rather shy and insecure about women. He's like the class clown in school who covers up his need for approval and his shyness with aggressive and offensive behavior. This type of man is actually rather easy to engage. And when it happens, this man trusts and loves quite readily.

"I don't want someone who is shy! I have enough trouble feeling confident in myself—I sure don't want to have to prop up some guy. I want someone who is confident and sure of himself." Feelings such as these are not uncommon; but remember, men who create exciting first impressions often direct their energy toward perfecting flash, not substance and follow-through.

Because sensitive men experience the same fears and vulnerabilities women do, they often reveal themselves slowly. Some amount of trust and familiarity must be established before they will allow themselves to be seen. Most women are acutely aware of their own sensitivities and insecurities and know the kinds of situations that allow them to feel safer and freer. But many women think that men operate with a quite different set of emotions. They may not see men as susceptible to feeling vulnerable—at least not in the way women do. Some women don't even like to consider this possibility! Many women believe that it is easy and natural for men to be outgoing and aggressive, and that is simply not true. Some men need an accepting or supportive atmosphere to reveal dormant aspects of their personality.

Andrew, a painfully shy 46-year-old physicist who loves his work, is definitely not a powerhouse with the ladies. Ellen, a high school teacher, had dated him only a few times when she began to feel bored and disinterested. But instead of ending the relationship, she decided to attempt to draw this man out. She made a game of it, being light, humorous, and spontaneous in his company. He responded immediately, revealing a wit and confidence that had been inhibited. Only then did the real "chemistry" occur. They are now quite seriously and happily involved.

For every woman who as a girl spent hours by the phone waiting for some boy to call, there is a man who as a boy could not force his shaking fingers to dial the phone. The cultural expectation was for the boy to make the first move, and those first moves are the most intimidating, for they clearly declare attraction and desire and expose the initiator to rejection.

Men who most easily overcame that boyhood fear were those who were the least in touch with their own feelings—or anyone else's. So those men who seem, in the beginning, most strong, interesting, and attractive may also be less complex, sensitive, and loving than those who initially appear less captivating.

But before a woman can truly appreciate the diamond in the rough, she has to examine the criteria according to which she evaluates men. She may have to throw out some old and useless stereotypes about "nice" or "gentle" being synonymous with "weak" and may need to bring such needs as security, consistency, commitment, and comfort closer to the top of her list of priorities with men.

It's interesting that when women are asked to describe what attracted them to men, they often talk about excitement or electricity. But when they are asked what is important in a relationship, they without exception remember the most tender and intimate moments. These substantive experiences are the important and essential ingredients in a good and lasting relationship, and yet women may overlook them, especially in the beginning when they are quickly deciding whether to take the time to get to know the other person.

Take a chance. Take a second or even a third look at that man you are tempted to ignore. Try spending a bit of time with him, keeping your mind free of expectations. You might find that you can enjoy not feeling nervous—that it's better feeling comfortable. You might let him tell you about himself slowly, in the same way you feel most at ease revealing yourself to him. You may even discover, to your surprise, that you like him.

Reinvesting in Long-Term Relationships

The suggestions we have offered in this chapter arise partly out of our observing a major shift in attitude among women today. It definitely appears that women are entering the era of the diamond in the rough—a time in which women are reinvesting in the value of solid and durable relationships.

Social upheavals in the recent past encouraged women to redefine themselves and aspire to their best. In order to pursue careers and self-actualization, many women placed the importance of relationships on hold and, along with it, the diamond in the rough. One reason was that the diamond in the rough was not seen as the sort of man who perhaps best symbolized the height of self-realization. Women may have passed him over for the most elusive man who appeared to be a more fitting match and more appropriate "achievement."

But now, many women are coming to believe that a career in the absence of a relationship can be a hollow and empty experience. So there is a swing back to a new balance or equilibrium in one's personal needs. Excitement and electricity may be wonderful while dating, but women today now want to connect more deeply with men and are eager to marry and have children.

This shift in focus from oneself to a more complex context, such as family, requires a rearrangement of values and selection criteria. This larger context of marriage and family suggests that many women are starting to look for men who are clearly solid, reliable, and trustworthy.

The smart woman who complained that she always fell for the rat is starting to look at men in new ways, viewing different kinds of men as possible "gems." Perhaps some women reading this may be thinking that this woman is merely desperate and willing to compromise in order to escape those lonely evenings. Nothing could be further from the truth. We are not referring to women who are settling for "crumbs" or second best, but women who are finding new value in men they would have discarded in the past. When asked, they themselves feel they are not "settling for" but "getting smart." These women sense a new level of appreciation of certain men, and because of that they feel they have a broader range of options, which is, in fact, exciting. Breaking away from narrow and rigid standards is a liberating experience for them.

Kathleen, in her late thirties, has had scores of relationships, most of which ended in painful dissolutions. "I had to take a fresh look at what I was really searching for. I found that when I went slowly and gave it a chance, I cared in a way that I never had before. It wasn't flash, glitter, and chemistry, but it feels even better than what I had in the past. I don't know whether I just got tired or what, but I feel good now and hopeful."

We predict that many women are adopting and will continue to adopt Kathleen's attitude. Furthermore, we fully believe that if women at least try to adopt it, they will find themselves in new and very rewarding relationships.

CHAPTER TWELVE

A Fresh Look at "Femininity"

Some women always seem to come out winners with men. There is a quality these women exude that can be so powerful and attractive that men appear mesmerized by them. What they have is the ability to be both tender and giving, as well as strong and powerful. They reject any narrow rigid stereotype of "femaleness." These women have no sense of compromising either aspect of their personality. For them, allowing both the so-called male and so-called female forces to reach full expression represents a magical balance that creates a kind of "synergy," an energy that is greater than the sum of the two forces.

What we see happening today with women

is a new definition of femininity that is closer to this balance of positive forces. And we find many smart women today starting to reexamine this basic aspect of their identity. They are asking themselves, "can I be strong, fully realized intellectually, and express the forceful dynamic parts of my personality in the presence of men and still be seen as desirable by these men?" This latter point is critical for men and women. We want the opposite sex to be attracted to us without having to censor or diminish any of the personal qualities which we value in ourselves.

We don't feel that it is a negative for men or women to be concerned with what the opposite sex values as "attractive." Rather, we believe it is important for both sexes to acknowledge that their definitions of "attractiveness" or masculinity and femininity are always partially defined by the opposite sex. We need to attract each other—it is a biological imperative.

As Carol Gilligan has noted, because attraction and connection seem to be of great importance to women, it is only natural that they focus on that which attracts men. The critical issue is to do this without sacrificing energy and integrity from other aspects of self-realization.

What does femininity mean? The traditional definition connoted passivity, weakness, delicacy, and girlishness. It placed fundamental importance upon appearance and presentation and implied coyness, coquettishness, disguises, games, and strategies. Today, femininity is being redefined simply as the quality of being uniquely female or womanly. Specifically, it refers not only to those qualities one traditionally associates more with women than men—tenderness, sensitivity, and nurturance—but also includes behaviors that tradition links more with men—strength, power, and aggressiveness. In fact, this broadened definition of womanliness is already being embraced by increasing numbers of women. These women are learning that being strong and assertive does not detract from feeling womanly, but rather complements such feelings. They also understand that expressions of strength don't rob them of their capacity to be tender and giving.

The Magic of Strength and Tenderness

We all have female and male aspects in our personalities. This is a common way of understanding our different personality traits. For example, there is the Eastern concept of Yin and Yang, masculine and feminine opposites which form a complementary whole. The psychologist Carl Jung spoke of the *anima* and the *animus* in describing the feminine and masculine that exist, in combination, in all of us.

As we've indicated, concepts of feminity and masculinity have come under considerable fire in recent years, and for some very good reasons. The restrictiveness of learned sexual role behaviors has been destructive to both women and men. Assertiveness was often systematically discouraged in girls and women, as were the expressions of tenderness and vulnerability in boys and men. Instead of feeling comfortable with rigid definitions of our sexual identities, many of us felt they were constraining. Women and men wanted to be "more" than what traditional sexual stereotypes called acceptable or appropriate. Such stereotypes were seen as straitjackets, restraints that choked off valuable parts of one's potential.

For women, a large part of the problem was that these role restraints said as much about what a woman shouldn't be or do as they did about what was expected of her. And it was those "don'ts" that particularly offended women. No one—man or woman—wants to have important expressions of his or her personality cut off, held back, or contaminated by embarrassment or shame. It is as basically natural and healthy for women to exercise their power

and forcefulness as it is for men to express
tenderness. In our experience, women who develop the most vital, interesting, and satisfying relationships with men are those who have
learned to express the masculine and feminine
aspects of their personalities in the fullest way
possible. Women who allow both to be expressed
can be gentle, nurturing, and sexy, as well as
firm, aggressive, and forceful.

Some women still believe it is the overtly
sexy, flirtatious, or submissive woman who is
most successful with men. This is not true at
all. It is true that sexy or flirtatious behavior
may catch a man's interest at first, but that
hook does not hold for long. Something more
powerful, basic, and intense has to happen.

What a man is attracted to most deeply in a
woman is a magical mixture of unadulterated
power and tenderness—in equal measure. Many
women have felt it necessary to hide the clear
expression of their strength until recently for
fear that men would be threatened by it, see
them as "ballsy," and be turned off. Fortunately, women said, "The hell with it," and
began expressing strengths and stretching themselves despite what men might think.

As women broke free of restrictive sexual
stereotypes, as they enjoyed flexing their mus-
cles in positive and growing ways, many also
became somewhat self-conscious about their

giving, nurturing sides. Instead of seeing these wonderful qualities as solid pluses, they frequently interpreted them as weaknesses.

The fallacy in this thinking is that those characteristics typically associated with women never reflected weakness in the first place. Strength, forcefulness, and mastery can be gained without giving up female tenderness and concern with relationships. All these attributes can coexist. It is this very rich and complete combination that is the greatest and most lasting turn-on for men.

There are some women who have always known how to make men fall for them. They have known it from the time they were little girls. They know it intuitively, but it's not linked to a secret gene; it's the result of astute observation and the ability to make good use of those observations. These women like being women, and they like men. They are as comfortable with their sensuality as they are with their strength; they trust in their tenderness and are confident in their power.

What do these women who combine strength and softness communicate to a man? What precisely is their allure? Here is what different men told us:

"My wife is also my best friend. There is no one I'd rather go to a movie or be on a trip with than her . . .. She's been a better and more loyal friend than anyone else."

"Women are easier to talk to about personal things—I don't know whether they are more understanding, or whether I just feel more comfortable opening up with them."

"I like women who can be tender to the extreme but who don't let me get away with anything. I like a woman who has the courage to be direct and forceful and the wisdom to be gentle and caring."

"The reason I'm in love with Cathy is that she has her own career and she's also very caring with me. I feel as if I have everything. She really understands what it's like to be anxious at work even though I'm basically a very confident guy."

"The greatest turn-on for me is a woman who is smart and knows it. She keeps the relationship alive. I like listening to her stories about her job at the end of the day. After the initial phase of a relationship, I used to get really bored being the only one to talk. There's nothing more boring to me than listening to myself."

"I think the best women are both bright and funny. If you have a sense of humor, you have a soul and you can get through any life hassles."

"I resent women's thinking that men like dummies, bimbos, or airheads. I can't think of anything more depressing than meeting my lover at the end of the day and not being able to talk about what's happening to me, us, or the world. I need to be just as intellectually turned on with the woman in my life as with my male friends."

"Even though they can be maddening at times, I love women who are feisty and challenging. They bring out the best in me; I don't get bored because they keep me a little off guard. I get hooked on them, I feel alive, I love the banter and some, not all, of the unpredictability."

The combination of these strengths with a softness and empathic caring has an enormous impact upon men. Men feel secure with this kind of woman, grateful for the sense of partnership, and captivated by her warmth and giving.

The Courage to Express Yourself

Expressing strength can create anxiety for some women, as can expressing tenderness. Research has shown that some women may feel very apprehensive about being strong, assertive, or ambitious because they fear their power and autonomy will somehow cause them to be rejected. On the other hand, expressing softness can be difficult, too, because when a woman gives of herself freely, she is exposed, vulnerable to rejection, easily hurt. We have found that unless women are certain of their strength, they will not be confident in their ability to avoid old submissive traps as they explore their own softness. Expressing both strength and softness requires courage.

Change is often difficult, for it is hard for us to let down our defenses.

The only way to achieve a merger of the male and female forces within is first to become aware of any possible inner conflicts. Search inside and honestly ask yourself the following questions:

To what degree do I fear rejection for being strong?

To what extent do I worry about the impact of my strength on relationships?

How do I think a man would handle my strength if I expressed it freely?

How angry do I feel at having to worry about the possibility of being rejected by a man for being strong?

How comfortable do I feel letting my tenderness show in the presence of a man?

Do I feel my expressions of nurturance will be taken for granted, or, worse, exploited by a man?

The answers to these questions should reveal certain qualities that are more easily and more comfortably expressed than others. Obviously those "others" are important to concentrate upon and to gradually begin integrating into yourself. This process requires an attitude of experimentation and a willingness to actively distinguish between men's actual reactions to different aspects of yourself and what you may inaccurately fear men's reactions to be. Trying out new and different behaviors is never easy at first but can become more so with practice. The reward is a release of all the positive energies, excitement, strength, intellect, caring, warmth, and friendliness within you so that you will be free to form relationships with men that are rich and rewarding to the fullest.

One of the real blocks to new behavior is a feeling of "this is simply not me." As long as new behavior is relegated to that "not me" category, it will be just that. All of us have had fleeting fantasies of rewinding the tape and behaving more freely and confidently in a situation that made us nervous. In psychotherapy, that's called "visualization," the general idea of which is that you cannot act in a certain way unless you first believe you can do it. You must be able to visualize or picture yourself performing the action, like athletes who mentally imagine themselves breaking a record until they are finally able to do it.

To do the same thing with encounters with men you need to create a mental picture, too. Imagine yourself at a party or on a first date. Be creative and detailed in picturing the setting and a man. Be aware of the warmth and sensitivity you may sometimes inhibit for fear of feeling too vulnerable; be aware of your power and feelings of strength. Visualize yourself doing what is not usually a comfortable part of your most typical ways of relating with men. Remember, if you can't first picture yourself doing something, you definitely won't do it. Conjuring up or visualizing a new image of oneself is the first step toward actual change.

The second step in this learning process is rehearsal. In order to adopt a new style of behavior you have to express and experience it. The first time you try it, it may seem stilted and wooden. Don't despair. It's like the first time you tried to dance or serve a tennis ball. You probably felt awkward and embarrassed, but after some practice it became smooth and natural. Repetition reduces anxiety. New behaviors must be tried out before they can become a permanent part of our personality.

OVERCOMING SHYNESS ■ A barrier that is common to many of us but is a special obstacle to single men and women is shyness. Women who are smart with men are not less shy than others, but they did make a decision not to allow their shyness to dominate their life.

When you are feeling shy, you are painfully self-conscious. You feel the whole world is staring at you in a potentially critical or judgmental manner. One way to overcome this negative outlook is to imagine that the arrows of energy you feel are pointed at you are reversed—that they are coming from you and are directed toward others. At a party, when you walk into the room, take a deep breath and look around at *other* people—straight in the eye. Some people will look away because they also are shy; but others will continue to look because they are interested in you. You will appear self-confident, and, most important, you will begin to feel more self-assured and stronger.

TALKING TO MEN ▪ Another important aspect of full expression has to do with the way a woman typically talks to men. As we mentioned earlier, women often notice that when a man walks into a room where they are having a conversation with another woman, there are subtle but significant changes in posture, body language, even words. These changes are obviously related to habit and misconception, not necessity. Initially, they come from the self-consciousness of adolescence and the observation of how other girls altered their behavior when boys were around. These changes in behavior are often related to what some women think is appealing to men.

Part of a woman's learning how to express her own unique self more fully may involve learning how to talk to men in a different fashion—in the candid, "unedited" way she talks with her women friends. Men love women who can be relaxed and open with them. But it requires courage to trust that a revelation of how you think and feel is valuable, interesting, and acceptable to men. A woman's trust in herself and liking of herself have the effect of making men feel comfortable so that they are more likely to reveal *themselves* in honest, undefended ways.

The next time you are with a man, simply be aware (without acting differently) of what you might have talked about and how you might have expressed it had he been a woman instead of a man. You may be surprised at how frequently you leave things out or in other ways significantly modify your spontaneity or the completeness of your expressions.

By doing this, a woman can become acquainted with any tendency she may have to censor or edit what she reveals or, probably even more important, can realize what she *doesn't* reveal to men. The full expression of self can powerfully effect a positive change in even casual interactions with men.

CHAPTER THIRTEEN

What Smart Women Know

There are smart women who are also very smart with men. We have already examined the various beliefs and expectations that must be reevaluated to enable women to diminish the likelihood of making foolish choices. Now we would like to explore the "winning" attitudes that we believe are possessed by women who make smart choices.

The Adventure of Courtship

There are basic courting behaviors that evolve not necessarily from our conscious minds, but from years or even centuries of conditioning. Whether instinctual or not, one fact is clear: The male and female of the species have always pursued each other, often in studied or ritualized ways. For instance, it has been theorized that during the time of the ancient Egyptians, the real function of women's makeup was to entice men. Eye makeup was thought to create the illusion of dilated pupils and lipstick the illusion of a flush, both of which occur during sexual arousal. Many different forms of courting behavior or mating rituals have stood the test of time. From elements of appearance to elements of posturing to elements of more complexly organized behavior, courting is still primarily primitive and emotional.

The smart woman is aware of this. Women who manage to get the man they want do not dismiss or ignore the deep-rooted and primitive ways of attraction, enticement, and arousal. Instead, they take pleasure in them and evolve their own particular style of partaking in these rituals. The smart woman views dating and finding men as a kind of adventure.

One of the questions women most frequently ask us is "How do I learn to flirt?" Perhaps this seems like a silly question, but it's not, and it's definitely not asked by silly women. These women are really asking what it is that some women do that seems to attract men.

This behavior is generally characterized as "flirting" behavior. Obviously, it is not our task to prescribe particular ways of acting, nor would that even be useful, because the essence of flirting is simply the communication of an attitude. And those women who embrace the notion of dating and courting as a positive or delightful experience easily communicate that playful and receptive attitude to the men they meet.

Janice, a 29-year-old businesswoman, observes, "I used to dread dating. I used to stay in relationships long after they were interesting or even good for me just to avoid being out there again in the single world. I realized I felt nervous dating and meeting new people even though in a business meeting I could be tough and outgoing. I finally learned a great trick— how to reinterpret nervousness as excitement, which, at least for me, it really is. Now I look forward to meeting new men, and I've really come to enjoy that wonderful unspoken interplay that happens when I find a man I'm attracted to."

When courtship is viewed as an adventure, certain self-defeating tendencies diminish. For example, so often today, both men and women have a misguided notion that they should immediately be accepted for who they are and that therefore they "should" be uncompromising and unaccommodating during the initial stages of dating. Naturally, this rigidity prevents "chemistry" from occurring. Chemistry describes fitting or being in "sync" with each other, and it tends to happen when men and women are open and adventuresome rather than rigid.

Naomi, a 34-year-old film editor, says, "I've stopped being so defensive with men. It used to be that when I'd meet a guy, I would go in leading with my chin, determined not to be compromised in any way. I always came away feeling like I was respected but not much else. After I stopped preparing for battle, I relaxed, the man relaxed, and I started really enjoying myself."

Smart men and smart women allow an easy flow to occur when they first meet each other. Being relaxed, open, and receptive is not a violation of one's integrity—it's just being smart.

"Finding" Takes Initiative

The smart woman doesn't wait for good fortune; she creates it. She has learned that unless she has fun during the search it won't turn out well. Exploring new experiences with the opposite sex can be exciting and stimulating; in fact, the whole process can be an end in itself without one's becoming unduly apprehensive about eventual outcomes.

Many women find it helpful to date often, even with those men who are only mildly interesting to them at first. This helps reduce the nervousness which often accompanies meeting someone who arouses strong interest and attraction. The more contacts women have, the greater the range of experience and the more ease they feel during these adventures. Being single today requires this kind of open attitude. Meeting the right person is a numbers game—a matter of probabilities.

Smart women understand that meeting a man does not involve simply being in the "right place at the right time." It requires creating those situations. These women assume an active role in designing their lives in such a way as to enhance their chances of coming in contact with interesting men. They initiate conversations and communicate interest when they feel it, not holding back and waiting for the man to take the first step. While some men can be threatened or turned off by the intensity of some women's initial interest, most are flattered and put at ease by signs of a woman's attraction.

Women who are successful with men broaden their attraction standards and go out with many different types. They know that the more men they go out with, the more relaxed and spontaneous they become. Frequency of dating is a sure cure for nervousness.

Men Like Women Who Like Men

Women who genuinely like men somehow communicate this feeling, and they find that their warmth, interest, and acceptance are the best catalyst for creating chemistry. One simple definition of "chemistry" is the sense of delight one feels in the presence of another person. There are women who believe they must like men merely because they know they do not dislike or hate them. Obviously this is not enough. Nor is it sufficient merely to "need" men. You must actually like them in order to create an attractive aura. This certainly doesn't mean you will like all men, but smart women who want potential partners to feel comfortable with them have learned that it is important to develop an overall enjoyment and appreciation of the opposite sex.

We find that most women have not thought in any detail about whether or not they like men.

For women who wish to assess themselves in this area, here are some questions to think about:

Granted that men are very different from
women, do I like those differences?
What specifically do I like about men?
Do men need to be a particular way for me
to like them? What way or ways?
Is there anything I don't like about men? If
so, what specifically?
Do I like men or simply need them?
How comfortable do I feel in the company of
men who are not potential partners?
Do I have fun with men and enjoy spending
time with them?

If in answering these questions, you have
difficulty separating liking and enjoying men
from merely needing them, you have some work
to do. In order to "like" men, it is necessary to
go beyond fears and idealizations. You have to
go beyond your own insecurities. In short, you
have to learn to *accept* men.

Acceptance is a critical prerequisite to liking; liking follows emotional acceptance rather
than preceding it. Smart women like men after
they demystify them. They are able to do the
latter because they have developed a clear sense
of their own needs. Essentially, their emotional
life doesn't prevent them from seeing men
clearly.

One common block to accepting and liking
men is a lack of understanding. Many women

don't really understand men and therefore find it difficult to establish a genuine and comfortable liking of them. While women frequently think they understand men, much of what they "know" is determined by myth, cliché, and stereotype. It is difficult for men and women to understand one another fully, for it is often threatening for us to either see the full, unadorned picture or to reveal it to ourselves. For many people, it is easier to view others in convenient but overgeneralized and inaccurate stereotypes.

Men play an active and self-defeating part in perpetuating male stereotypes and mythology. They don't typically present themselves as needing or wanting to be understood—even though they do. Their own insecurities are directed toward preventing women from seeing too much which would threaten and undermine their own belief systems about masculinity.

What many women fail to understand about men lies in the area of male vulnerability and sensitivities which we have already explored. This area includes important unspoken fears of helplessness and passivity, of entrapment, of dependency, and of not being able to live up to the woman's idealized image of the man.

Men need to be liked, loved, and respected in spite of their vulnerabilities. Those men who sense a real acceptance and understanding of them and the liking that follows along return that care and respect to the women who give it.

Men Respond to Sensitivity

Once smart women develop a relationship, how do they keep it alive? First, they have learned how to create a context in which the man can allow his needs to emerge and be expressed within the relationship. Whether men admit it or not, most of them enjoy needing a woman. Having established this most basic bond, these women understand how to sustain the positive "tension" so necessary to keep relationships alive.

In the initial stages of a relationship, a man may hold back in certain ways until trust develops, even though he really does want an intimate partner. Most men today experience a great deal of stress and pressure. They need someone to talk to, someone with whom they feel comfortable unburdening themselves. But when men are under pressure, much of their talk can be tedious and repetitious even though they themselves are afraid of being seen as whiny and complaining. So when men find women who listen and can understand them, these women are found to be irresistible. Men want to be with women with whom they can express themselves openly and feel no danger of being judged harshly.

Some women are wary of a man who needs to unburden himself. Such women can be afraid that this type of man could be weak and thus unable to reciprocate when her needs are pressing. In the initial part of a relationship this should not be cause for concern, since there is plenty of time to assess a man's strengths and weaknesses. It is probably more important to be aware of the man who does not express his concerns, for he typically is unable to trust others.

Cameron, a 35-year-old sound engineer, describes a current relationship: "Until I met Carolyn, I always held back with women. I don't know whether I really had to, but I felt like I had to, and the net result was the same. With Carolyn it's all different. I'm not sure exactly what she does that's all that different, but I can talk to her about anything. I can't tell you what a relief it is to find a woman I can actually open up to and be myself with."

When she is with a man, the smart woman often listens to what is going on beneath the words in their conversations. Frequently a throwaway line, or perhaps some grumbling about work, is in truth an attempt on the part of a man to reveal something that is deeply troubling him. When anyone, man or woman, experiences career problems, fears of failure, or financial anxieties, the concern is not a superficial one. The man who sees a woman as someone he knows will understand and be helpful feels blessed and is not likely to look elsewhere to get his needs met.

Whether it be career concerns or cues picked up about other areas of worry, insecurity, or vulnerability, men appreciate a woman's sensitivity and acceptance. We all need to feel at ease with as many facets of our personality and life situation as possible. Sensitivity to each other, particularly in areas of intimate personal concern, is a wonderful gift.

Vital Relationships: The Paradox of Romantic Tension and Love

There are some important differences between men and women when it comes to romance. Though not consciously, men tend to divide relationships into the courting and capture phases. Those behaviors associated with courtship diminish after the capture. Men are romantic during the hunt and can be wonderfully charming, thoughtful, and sensitive. Their attention to detail is heightened during this time. They are more sensitive to a woman's feelings and needs and may send her flowers or a loving card the day after a romantic date. But after the capture, when they sense the woman cares, they change. They subtly but definitely shift their focus away from romance and toward security, trust, and closeness. They once again turn back to the world and their work for attention and excitement, and thus drift away from the intensity of romance.

Women tend to be different. They want romance to continue and are disappointed when it ceases. Women often feel "taken for granted" by men when romantic behavior fades. While for most men romance is a means to an end, to many women it is an end in itself. Most women don't feel discomfort with romance; they love it. Men, on the other hand, are anxious to get beyond the pursuit so they can stop worrying, relax, and enjoy the rewards of victory. Whereas women tend to equate pursuit with love, men equate not having to pursue with love!

What a dilemma! Is there no hope for romance? Of course there is. A committed relationship need not be a life without passion or the unexpected. If you are a woman who wants to keep a man behaving in a romantic fashion or to rekindle that active interest, don't push him to go to more musicals or on that intimate picnic. If you keep pushing him, you will probably succeed in making him feel pressured and guilty, but you surely aren't going to get him to feel more romantic. Even if he gives in and dutifully brings home a dozen roses from the florist shop, it will be mere compliance. And the smart woman knows that compliance is an enemy of romance. The smart thing to do is simply to allow him to enjoy being loved. Interpret his diminished need to be romantic as a compliment, as a hallmark of his trust and belief in your love.

"Who cares about how he feels, how comfortable he is? I want romance!" Well, there is a solution. Your first step is to understand and master an important psychological law that smart women know—partial reinforcement. Partial reinforcement means rewarding a person for certain behavior some of the time but not all the time. If a laboratory rat is rewarded with a feed pellet every time he presses a bar, he will work quite hard. But he will work much harder at bar pressing if he is rewarded only at odd intervals. Uncertainty causes him to work harder. He will press like a demon if he doesn't know exactly when he will be rewarded.

Uncertainty also works with men. For example, a woman who breaks dates with a man a couple of times or comes home late and is slightly vague will drive him absolutely nuts. The uncertainty it stimulates in him would motivate him to reembark on romantic ventures.

Remember, for men romance is goal-oriented behavior, a time when men are uncertain of a woman's feelings toward them. The key word is "uncertainty." During this time men are most concerned with how they look, what they weigh, how they dress. When men are uncertain, they shave on weekends, dress more carefully, and invest in after-shave lotion. And, of course, most important, when men are uncertain, they find themselves becoming more romantic.

One woman says, "I've learned that the best way to ensure romantic behavior from men is to keep them just ever so slightly off balance. I'm a little less available than I normally would be or I'll go out to a movie with a friend—maybe even have a drink afterward, and when I get home be just a bit vague. I really do love the man I'm with, and I wouldn't do anything to hurt or betray him. But it's fun to keep a little mystery in the relationship. He says he hates it, but he acts like he loves it."

Now, you may consider all this to be some silly game you don't want to play. Why should you have to create uncertainty to spark interest from a man? Why should it be your obligation to keep the relationship magical and alive? Well, it's not your obligation, and you needn't do any of this. Certainly it would be ideal if you and the man in your life could sit down and tell each other what you need and expect to get. But in the real world, unfortunately, things don't always work that way. There really is nothing wrong with viewing the dance between men and women as involving some strategy. We are not speaking of manipulative behavior but about mating rituals. Smart men and women keep each other both interested and stimulated. Smart women do not allow themselves to be lulled into forgetting there is a balance of ease, security, and tension that keeps a relationship alive.

Having accepted that uncertainty, in varying degrees, is invaluable in a relationship, what are the ways in which this attitude can be implemented? The key concept is not losing sight of your own sense of autonomy and self-reliance. When a woman out of love, habit, or need begins to mold or shape her life-style around the man, no matter how loving her motivation, she has a very specific effect on him. He doesn't have to wonder about her—he experiences no uncertainty. While certainty can feel reassuring some of the time, it also means his wonderment and curiosity about her will begin to wane.

We would like to present some suggestions that lead to positive outcomes but which still allow the woman to maintain her own individuality even while continuing to stimulate curiosity and intrigue in a man. The following are behaviors and attitudes that can maintain that marvelous tension between love and uncertainty.

TRUSTING AND EXPRESSING ONESELF

■ Get to know your own likes and dislikes, and make sure to bring them into the relationship. When a man experiences this in a woman, it makes him feel she's unique and stimulating enough so that a sense of surprise and interest will be maintained in their relationship. Men tell us that women's needs for them to "take charge" and be the initiator can ultimately be burdensome. So remember to please yourself, not just the man. Don't make him the central focus. When a man feels he's the focus, it is momentarily flattering, but ultimately boring. The more confident and self-assured a person, the more interesting he is. Today, men often express a sense of tedium at hearing their own "stories" over and over. For example, Bob notes how seldom his dates will change the flow of conversation. "I'm surprised how often women seem to feel that asking about my life and career is interesting. I really enjoy women who like to talk about their interests and dreams."

PRIVACY IS NOT BAD ▪ Too much "openness" can be a turn-off. Respect for one's privacy does not preclude intimacy. Endless "honest and open" dialogues about the way you feel about each other can even serve to disguise a fear of separateness. Further, they can constrict and dilute that special joy of slowly getting to know each other. Privacy, in fact, can provide reservoirs of future knowledge about each other that serve to maintain a sense of newness. Gradual revelations of ourselves serve to enhance positive tension and heighten the promise of mutual discoveries. Many men find they are intrigued by women who maintain areas of privacy.

CONTAINING INSECURITY ▪ It is important to contain, to some degree, your insecurity and your need for security. We have covered this elsewhere but it bears repeating. Men can feel overwhelmed by these disclosures, and delightful uncertainty becomes replaced, in their minds, by becoming certain they will be depleted or drained. Men are relieved when women feel confident and desirable enough so that they are not anxiously and prematurely evaluating the man's potential for commitment and marriage.

MAINTAINING SEPARATE INTERESTS ▪ Sharing common interests is valuable in any relationship, but too much togetherness can be dull. Separate interests lead to separate experiences, and it is these separate experiences that create newness and stimulation. While we all desire a mate to appreciate and enjoy what is special to us, it is also exciting to be led into new experiences.

AVOIDING THE ROUTINE ■ Ruts occur when we let ourselves down, when we don't allow the unexpected to emerge in our conversations or what we do. Experimentation and risk-taking prevent the onset of that dreaded kiss of death—predictability. So take a chance, throw yourself a curve ball in relating to a man. Trust that his being off balance can be intriguing and challenging to him. As one man put it, "I actually love it that just when I thought I really knew her, she comes up with a totally unexpected point of view or interest."

If we had to express these suggestions in an equation, it would go something like this: Being your own person = Not worrying what the man thinks = Spontaneity = Unpredictability = Uncertainty = The right amount of vital tension and love which serves to enliven relationships.

Men Do Commit

There is a myth that men today run from commitment.

We believe this is nonsense. Just as women do, more men than ever before want involvement and marriage—including men who have been married before. In fact, those previously married men typically don't stay single for long. What may appear to women as resistance to commitment in men is actually a thin veneer of caution—men today are as eager as women are to enter into intimate relationships employing traditional values. We all desire a nest for ourselves, and smart women know this applies to men as well as to themselves.

It has been our experience that one of the more poorly understood aspects of a man's bond with a woman is his need for her. In his own way, he may attempt to hide it or disguise it in hopes she will not notice. In turn, some women feel discomfort with a man's dependency, a fact which may cause him to disguise the intensity of his need for her. The net result is that many women are not fully aware of male dependency and as a result do not realize the leverage and power they possess. To the extent that you may need to see the man in your life as powerful and capable of protecting you,

you may be blind to his need for you. Few men will say, "I can't live without you." Yet the majority who are deeply involved with a woman actually feel that way. You may have met a man who didn't seem to fit this pattern. But these men may have disengaged after they were nagged or cajoled for months or years to make a commitment. And just as quickly they fell for someone else. That is not how you do it. You don't nag, complain, or get angry. You have to be firm in a way that comes from your heart.

Tessa, a 36-year-old bank loan officer, was convinced that Larry, a man with whom she had been involved for nearly two years, would never make a final decision to marry her. He had been married previously, as had she, but he seemed more scarred from the experience and continued to have painful and frustrating interactions with his ex-wife, usually involving their two children. Tessa was outwardly patient and understanding with Larry, logging countless hours of listening to him express his concerns, frustrations, and angers. Tessa also felt loved by Larry, who was warm, affectionate, and giving in every area except when it came to that final gift—his commitment to her.

She was aware that her patience was sliding toward the edge of annoyance and disbelief even though she did understand the reasons for his caution and need to "be sure and not make another mistake." As Tessa recalls, "I told him I was at the point where I knew it had to move forward or I was going to start resenting him, and I loved him too much to let that happen. I started to cry, and so did Larry. Larry knew this wasn't a threat—he saw my pain and the impending negative turn our relationship would take. A day later, he told me he wanted to get married."

Smart women can reduce a man's resistance by giving him a positive ultimatum. "Listen, you son of a bitch, the party's over" is not what we mean here. That's a threat fueled by anger and frustration. A positive ultimatum goes something like this: "I feel we've been together long enough to make a permanent commitment. I love you and I want us to be together—always. I know you're unsure, but I want you to make a decision within three months. I'm saying this out of love and a desire to keep things as wonderful as they are. Otherwise, I'll be miserable, begin to nag you, and make both of us crazy, and then our relationship will sour." When you feel a relationship is terrific and you've been together long enough to know that he does too, you may have to be the one who gets him to make some important decisions.

Sometimes ultimatums are necessary, and

they are effective. Men don't let go of women they love and need. They run away from women who complain and grind away. Do it cleanly. It's not brinkmanship, it's reality. Don't let your cherished relationship be eroded by bitterness or passive wishful thinking.

The Smart Woman Is Responsible for Her Own Experience

The smart woman knows she is responsible for her experience in this world. She refuses to be a victim. She works hard at getting what she wants and needs.

The smart woman is strong and expects men to be able to deal with that strength. She has learned to communicate her needs early in the relationship, and if she sees the match as not fulfilling, she moves on. She doesn't hang on to misery or empty promises. The smart woman is not sitting at home staring at the phone, hoping it will ring. She goes after what she wants.

The smart woman likes herself, feels comfortable with herself, and likes men and her experiences with them. She understands thoroughly that she is a powerful determinant in what happens with men and herself. She is not angry or distrustful of individual men. Rather, she lets each experience determine a fresh new response. She doesn't expect perfection in a man or in herself. She can join with a man fully and with the total expression of her personality. But she never makes a man the center of her existence, for she has her own center.

The smart woman embraces her femininity and sexuality. She is not afraid to be sexy, for she understands its power to attract. Her sexuality is not self-conscious; it comes from within and is organic. It is not a role she puts on; it is a manifestation of her freedom and trust in the pleasure of being a woman and feeling womanly.

The smart woman moves toward experience. It isn't that she does not have concerns, insecurities, or anxieties; she simply has decided not to let them dominate her. Her orientation is toward understanding, not blaming. If she experiences a setback, she tries to make sense of it, then moves forward in her life.

These are some of the core components of what smart women know. They seek a path toward relationships that demand personal responsibility and clarity from themselves. The smart woman knows that all of us are entering a new time where we are discovering a renewed sense of delight in and appreciation for each other.

CHAPTER FOURTEEN

Rules for Finding the Right Man

In concluding this book, we would like to present a brief review of the fundamental rules that we believe a woman must fully understand and accept in order to stop making foolish choices and to get smarter with men.

RULE NUMBER ONE ■ *There are no perfect men.*

The perfect man is a romantic fiction. He doesn't exist. But there is a wondrous supply of really solid men out there. The desire to be swept away by a Prince probably derives from childhood hunger for Daddy.

RULE NUMBER TWO ■ *Exciting men can make women miserable.*

Women who confuse longing with love will pay a terrible price, because some men are afraid of genuine intimacy.

RULE NUMBER THREE ■ *Reforming a man is usually futile.*
Women have more rewarding things to do with their lives than make their lovers a lifetime "project."

RULE NUMBER FOUR ■ *Growing up means giving up Daddy.*
Men want an adult lover, a friend and partner—not a surrogate daughter. Childlike or manipulative women drive most men away.

RULE NUMBER FIVE ■ *Anger scares men off.*
Women who start new love affairs filled with old angers and resentments turn men off.

RULE NUMBER SIX ■ *No man can give a woman self-esteem.*
Men don't want to be counted on to rescue women or be their salvation. When they expect their mates to validate their self-worth as human beings, women set themselves up for anger, disappointment, and bitterness.

RULE NUMBER SEVEN ■ *Many good men go unnoticed.*

People's best qualities usually reveal themselves over time. Men with "flash" may be intriguing at first, but they frequently cannot give a woman sustained emotional nourishment.

RULE NUMBER EIGHT ■ *Fewer expectations lead to greater aliveness.*

An open, nonjudgmental attitude allows for delightful surprises in life. Men are wary of disguised expectations, and rigid "supposed to's" choke relationships.

RULE NUMBER NINE ■ *Fully realized women are strong and tender.*

Strength mingled with tenderness is a magic combination. The smart woman feels good about her womanliness. She trusts her strength and power enough to allow her tenderness to emerge.

RULE NUMBER TEN ■ *The game of courtship is delightful.*

Women who get the men they want don't fight mating rituals; rather they enjoy courtship within the context of their own particular style.

RULE NUMBER ELEVEN ■ *"Finding" takes initiative.*

The smart woman doesn't wait for good fortune, she creates it. She learns to enjoy the process of courting without undue focus on eventual outcomes.

RULE NUMBER TWELVE ■ *Men* like *women who like men.*

If you allow yourself to let men know you like them, they will sense it. This warmth and acceptance is the best catalyst for creating chemistry.

RULE NUMBER THIRTEEN ■ *Women who really listen are irresistible.*

Even if they don't admit it, most men enjoy needing a woman. They need someone to talk to, someone with whom they feel comfortable unburdening themselves, with no danger of being judged harshly.

RULE NUMBER FOURTEEN ■ *Romantic tension keeps relationships alive.*

In a relationship, we are most alive when we don't take our mate for granted. A little uncertainty keeps men stimulated and interested.

RULE NUMBER FIFTEEN ■ *Men* do *want to commit.*

It is a myth that men don't commit to relationships; they only appear that way. A smart woman is aware that the shock of an ultimatum may be what is needed to make a man aware.

RULE NUMBER SIXTEEN ■ *Women are responsible for their own experience.*

The smart woman is aware that she can create her own destiny and thus works hard at what she wants and needs.

Making smart choices—avoiding the wrong men and finding the right ones—requires a woman to have the courage to challenge within herself the beliefs and expectations that, while understandable, may have served to narrow her vision and opportunities. We have found these rules, when implemented, have a liberating effect and can enable a woman to create experiences with men that are refreshing as well as fulfilling.

APPENDIX

Quizzes and Tests

Patterns of Relationship Quiz

Put down on paper the names of the last five (or most important five) men with whom you have been romantically involved. Using the list of adjectives below, write in those that best characterize the men, in two columns for each man.

In the first column, list the adjectives that describe how you saw him in the beginning. In the second column, list the adjectives that best describe him at the end of the relationship.

adventurous	apprehensive	cautious
affluent	argumentative	changeable
aggressive	blunt	clever
altruistic	bold	compliant
anxious	calm	compromising
apologetic	carefree	critical

conventional	impulsive	secretive
cynical	inventive	self-conscious
defensive	intellectual	sensitive
defiant	inoffensive	shy
demanding	lighthearted	self-sacrificing
dependent	mellow	stern
domineering	methodical	strict
doubting	mild	stimulating
dynamic	modest	stubborn
egotistical	moralistic	skeptical
emotional	ordinary	sophisticated
excitable	opinionated	subtle
extravagant	outspoken	suspicious
extroverted	overeager	suggestible
forceful	overcritical	talkative
forward	polished	thrifty
funny	prudent	temperamental
guarded	philosophical	tough
happy-go-lucky	pessimistic	tender
headstrong	prominent	unassuming
humble	provocative	uncomplaining
hurried	religious	vain
idealistic	reserved	unpretentious
impatient	restless	witty
impersonal	scrappy	worldly

Now, for each man listed, force yourself to choose only one response for each relationship. Write that entry under his name.

1. Looks
   a. Average, plain
   b. Rugged, masculine

c. Unusual-looking
d. Handsome
e. Cute, boyish

2. Masculine posture
   a. Macho veneer, but more flexible underneath it
   b. Rigidly masculine
   c. Neither masculine nor feminine
   d. A bit feminine

3. Family background
   a. Lower middle class
   b. Middle class
   c. Upper middle class

4. Education
   a. High school
   b. College degree
   c. Graduate or professional degree

5. Work
   a. Salaried employee
   b. Professional
   c. Self-employed

6. Income
   a. Under $30,000
   b. $30,000 to $60,000
   c. Over $60,000

7. Meeting
   a. Met through work
   b. Met through friends
   c. Accidental or chance meeting
   d. Bar or singles event
   e. Other (specify)

8. Future Orientation
   a. Neither of us were future-oriented about the relationship
   b. He was, I wasn't.
   c. I was, he wasn't.
   d. Both of us were future-oriented.

9. Caring
   a. He cared more for me.
   b. I cared more for him.
   c. There were no strong feelings either way.
   d. Caring was strong and equal.

10. Commonality of interests
    a. Little in common
    b. Some things in common
    c. Great deal in common

11. Values
    a. Greatly dissimilar values
    b. Little similarity in values
    c. Some values in common
    d. Most values the same

12. Intensity of need
   a. There was little intense need on either part.
   b. I needed him more.
   c. He needed me more.
   d. We both needed each other strongly.

13. Depth of love
   a. I loved him more.
   b. He loved me more.

14. Commitment
   a. He was more committed.
   b. I was more committed.

15. Change
   a. We accepted each other fairly well.
   b. I wanted him to change in important ways.
   c. He wanted me to change in important ways.
   d. Both of us had major complaints and wishes for the other to change.

16. How early was trouble detected?
   a. I knew from early on that the relationship wouldn't work.

   b. We had a long period during
      which everything worked
      well.
   c. I didn't know until the end
      that there was anything
      wrong.

17. How long did you stay
     knowing it wouldn't work?
   a. I left as soon as I knew.
   b. I left, but not nearly as soon
      as I should have.
   c. I stayed much too long.

18. The break-up
   a. I precipitated the break-up.
   b. He did.
   c. It was basically a mutual
      decision.

Now, look for the patterns, similarities, and what you learned from the men and about yourself from each relationship.

Love Addiction Test
Answer the following questions true or false:

	True	False
1. I don't seem to find myself very "good company" or enjoy spending time alone when I have free evenings.	☐	☐

2. When someone inquires about my love life, I sometimes feel uncomfortable letting him know I am available. □ □

3. I find myself daydreaming a lot about men, particularly the ones I can't have. □ □

4. Even though it's hard to admit, I know the only thing that could ever make me truly happy is having a man. □ □

5. Most of the time I'm not able to enjoy going out to eat or to the movies alone. □ □

6. I worry about the amount of time I spend fantasizing about men. □ □

7. I tend to avoid going to social gatherings when I know almost all the people there will be couples. □ □

8. I'm aware that when I'm involved with a man it's the only time I feel secure inside. □ □

9. Even though it annoys my friends, I'm likely to change plans with them if I get a last-minute invitation from a man. □ □

10. I know I spend much too much time devising plans and strategies designed to "get a man." ☐ ☐

11. My feeling of self-worth and general well-being really goes up when I have a man in my life and dips sharply when I don't have a man around. ☐ ☐

12. When it comes to men, "the grass always seems to be greener" and I'm never really satisfied. ☐ ☐

13. I'm an insatiable reader of romance novels. ☐ ☐

14. I seem to find myself moving from one infatuation to another. ☐ ☐

15. I hate to admit it, but I find that yearning for a man is much more interesting and romantic than feeling sure of a man's love. ☐ ☐

16. Somehow my life never really seems okay unless there is a man to share it with. ☐ ☐

17. I feel much more excited when I'm doing the loving than when a man is going out of his way to love me. ☐ ☐

18. I lose interest in my work and even other activities that are normally important to me when I'm not involved with a man. □ □

19. The only time I ever really feel alive is when I'm with a man. □ □

20. I do want a lasting relationship and to settle down. But every time I meet the man whom I think that will happen with, I find one thing or another about him that seems to turn me off. □ □

SCORING AND INTERPRETING THE TEST
Add up all of the items marked True.

0 True items: If none of the items were marked True, you have a healthy way of looking at yourself independent of your relationships with men. You show no tendency toward love addiction.

1–3 True items: If you marked *even one* item True, you place some excessive concern, importance, or need upon the idea of having a man in your life. You do have some of the warning signs of becoming a love addict.

4–7 True items: If you checked at least four items True, you are struggling with love addiction. It may not yet be apparent to you, but the importance you place upon men and love is within the red zone for love addiction.

Over 7 True items: If you marked at least seven items as True, you already know you are a love addict. This is a serious addiction and will require an equally serious commitment to "breaking the habit."

Satisfaction of Needs Test

HOW TO TAKE THE TEST
Listed below are six broadly defined categories of personal needs. Each category is made up of a number of specific needs. These needs range from ways you would like to feel to how you would like to be treated in a relationship. No one need see how you score this test, so be as honest with yourself as possible. This is not a test of wishes and dreams, but rather a way to look at things the way they are.

You will notice that beside each need described below are two columns of blanks. Using the rating scales, choose the number that best fits the intensity of your personal need. Place that number in the left-hand column to the right of the need described. Now, for the same need, choose the number that best fits the frequency with which the need is met in your relationships. That number goes in the right-hand column. In this way, rate each of the personal needs described.

Remember, we're talking about how these needs are met or not met *in your relationship*.

RATING SCALES

Left-hand column	*Right-hand column*
No Need (1)	Not Met (1)
Little Need (2)	Infrequently Met (2)
Moderate Need (3)	Moderately Met (3)
Important Need (4)	Frequently Met (4)
Extremely Important Need (5)	Almost Always Met (5)

Excitement and Challenge Needs

1. Opportunity to take personal risks   ___ ___
2. Need for some sense of danger or thrill   ___ ___
3. Need for novelty and change   ___ ___
4. Need for challenge and mastery   ___ ___
5. Need for stimulation   ___ ___
6. Need to be kept slightly off balance or "on my toes"   ___ ___
7. Need for some sense of intrigue or mystery   ___ ___

Autonomy Needs

  8. Need for emotional independence   ____   ____

  9. Need for financial independence   ____   ____

10. Need for personal freedom   ____   ____

11. Need for equality   ____   ____

12. Need for mutuality and reciprocity   ____   ____

13. Need for roles defined by interest and aptitude, not by gender   ____   ____

14. Need for solitude and alone time without him wondering what is wrong   ____   ____

15. Need for privacy   ____   ____

16. Need for control   ____   ____

Security Needs

17. Need to feel protected
     (a) Physically
     (b) Emotionally
     (c) Financially

18. Need for trust in mate   ____   ____

19. Need to be trusted by mate   ____   ____

20. Need for familiarity and security   ____   ____

21. Need for predictability from mate   ____   ____

22. Need for continuity and mutual goals   ____   ____

23. Need for approval   ____   ____

24. Need to be controlled   ____   ____

25. Need for comfort and safety   —— ——
26. Need for sharing and common experience   —— ——

Sexual and Affection Needs

27. Need for personal sexual expression without inhibition   —— ——
28. Need for mate to be sexually expressive without inhibition   —— ——
29. Need for monogamy   —— ——
30. Need for nonsexual affection (not simply a prelude to sexual activity)   —— ——
31. Need for sexual novelty and variety of sexual expression   —— ——
32. Need for verbal expressions of caring and tenderness   —— ——
33. Need for variety of sexual partners   —— ——
34. Need to give nurturance and feel it is valued   —— ——
35. Need to receive nurturance from mate   —— ——

Communication Needs

36. Need for clear and direct communication   —— ——
37. Need for personal emotional expression   —— ——

38. Need for emotional expression from mate   ____   ____
39. Need for intimacy and closeness   ____   ____
40. Need for discussion of all issues important to me   ____   ____
41. Need for discussion of issues important to mate   ____   ____
42. Need for mutual openness   ____   ____
43. Need for personal disclosure   ____   ____
44. Need for personal disclosure from mate   ____   ____

Feeling State Needs

45. Need for personal respect from mate   ____   ____
46. Need to feel loved   ____   ____
47. Need to feel essential or needed by mate   ____   ____
48. Need to feel appreciated by mate   ____   ____
49. Need for some sense of longing for mate   ____   ____
50. Need to feel supported emotionally by mate   ____   ____
51. Need to feel encouraged to grow by mate   ____   ____
52. Need for feelings of jealousy   ____   ____
53. Need to feel respect for mate   ____   ____
54. Need for feelings of acceptability (lack of critical judgment from mate)   ____   ____

SCORING AND INTERPRETING THE TEST

Add the numbers in columns 1 and 2. It may be helpful to look at which general categories of needs have the largest discrepancies.

1. Individual need scores where left-hand and right-hand columns are the same or where the left-hand column is less than the right-hand column indicate no conflict.

2. In looking at the various categories of needs, categories that don't reflect large discrepancies between the columns are likewise relatively conflict-free.

3. In looking at individual items, if the left-hand column is at least 2 points higher than the right-hand column, it is significant.

In interpreting this test, what you will be looking for are discrepancies between the needs you bring to a relationship and how well they're met. In addition to noting the overall score of dissatisfaction or satisfaction, look at the various categories to see if there are particular areas where you have difficulty finding fulfillment.

In examining the results you can adopt one of two attitudes. If you want to be a "blamer" you can hold men responsible for the discrepancies or dissatisfactions, or you can examine, as we suggest you do, your own responsibility or unrealistic expectations. This test can indicate where your needs may be excessive or whether you're looking for the wrong kind of man. For example, a "nice guy" could meet almost all of your needs except the "excitement" ones. The solution: Count your blessings and take up skydiving.

1. If the overall total for the left-hand column is less than the total for the right-hand column, most of your needs are being met in the context of the relationship. You are luckier than anyone we know—don't you dare let him out of your sight.

2. If the left-hand column is more than the right-hand column

By 1–25 points: Count yourself among the most fortunate. It's a minor miracle that so many needs can be met in a relationship with anyone.

By 26–50 points: Reflects good solid relationship with most needs being met.

By 51–75 points: Reflects the presence of potentially important differences. Such differences are not overwhelming and may be sharply reduced by clearer communication with your partner. It also may require more boldness on your part to negotiate your needs.

By 76–100 points: Differences as large as these indicate significant problems. Many of your important needs are not being met. This failure may be due to poor communication and understanding or it may well be more serious. It may very well reflect unrealistic expectations or a poor choice in men.

By 100 or more points: With differences as consistent and widespread as this score suggests, your relationships are in real trouble. Either your partners are turkeys, or you are incredibly foolish in your expectation that such excessive needs can be met in any relationship.

About the Authors

Dr. Connell Cowan and Dr. Melvyn Kinder are in private practice in Los Angeles, California. Any communications to the authors should be addressed to:

Dr. Connell Cowan
521 N. La Cienega Blvd.
Suite #15
Los Angeles, CA. 90048

Dr. Melvyn Kinder
521 N. La Cienega Blvd.
Suite #209
Los Angeles, CA. 90048